Strategies for Success on the SAT:
Critical Reading & Writing Sections

Contributing Author:

Lauren Meggison, M.A., M.F.A., Ph.D.
B.A., College of Creative Studies, University of California, Santa Barbara
    (double major in English and Art)
M.F.A., Writing (Fiction Program), University of California, Irvine
M.A., Comparative Literature, University of California, Irvine
Ph.D., Comparative Literature, University of California, Irvine
Former Instructor and Lecturer, Literature & Writing, Humanities Department,
    University of California, Irvine
Director, Cambridge Academic Services & Consulting, Inc. and the *Lyceum for Elementary Enrichment & Test Prep*
    (4th – 6th grades), Laguna Beach, California

Acknowledgements:

iUniverse: Susan Driscoll, Dan Silvia, Jessica Florez, Joyce Greenfield and Sally Peterson

FreelancePermissions.com: Natalie Giboney and Melissa Flamson

Avalon Marketing & Communications: Patty Lavelle

Kleinworks Agency: Judy Klein

The author expressly thanks Lauren Meggison for her contributions, dedicated assistance, and support. The author also gratefully acknowledges the contributions and efforts of Elisabeth Aulwurm, Michelle Ha, Y Thuan La, Evan Miyazono, Jennifer Owens, Nicole Edwards and Mariana Aguirre.

The author extends her deepest personal thanks to Maurice L. Muehle for his invaluable guidance and assistance.

Strategies for Success on the SAT:
Critical Reading & Writing Sections

by

Lisa Muehle

Director, Cambridge Academic Services & Consulting, Inc. and the *Colloquium Test Prep Course for the SAT*
(Long-term SAT training for 7th – 11th grade students)
Laguna Beach, California

iUniverse Star
New York Lincoln Shanghai

Strategies for Success on the SAT:
Critical Reading & Writing Sections

iUniverse Star
an iUniverse, Inc. imprint

iUniverse books may be ordered through booksellers or by contacting:

iUniverse
2021 Pine Lake Road, Suite 100
Lincoln, NE 68512
www.iuniverse.com
1-800-Authors (1-800-288-4677)

Because of the dynamic nature of the Internet, any Web addresses or links contained in this book may have changed since publication and may no longer be valid.

Further information:
Lisa Muehle, Director
Lauren Meggison, MFA, Ph.D., Director
Cambridge Academic Services & Consulting, Inc.
303 N. Broadway Plaza, Suite 204
Laguna Beach, California 92651
(949) 443-2700
www.e-cambridgetutors.com
E-mail: cambridge@e-cambridgetutors.com

ISBN: 978-1-58348-478-4 (pbk)
ISBN: 978-0-595-82550-9 (ebk)

Printed in the United States of America

The author gratefully acknowledges the following sources and appreciates permission granted to reprint material used in this book:

Pages 8 & 10: From GALE ENCYCLOPEDIA OF MEDICINE by John Thomas Lohr, Gale Group. © 1999, Gale Group. Reprinted by permission of The Gale Group.

Page 29: From *Wuthering Heights* by Emily Bronte. 1847.

Page 49: From "We'll miss you, Galileo" by James Ropp. www.physicspost.com. November 19, 2003. Reprinted by permission of the author.

Page 49: From "Lesson 11: The First Palaces in the Aegean," *The Prehistoric Archaeology of the Aegean*. http://projectsx.dartmouth.edu/history/bronze_age/. Reprinted by permission of Dr. Jeremy Rutter (Department of Classics, Dartmouth College).

Page 50: From "Rethinking Old Technology." www.infoplease.com. © 2004 Pearson Education, publishing as Information Please. Reprinted by permission.

Page 50: From "Jury Nullification" by Chuck Morse, City Metro Enterprises. www.chuckmorse.com. Reprinted by permission of Chuck Morse – World Net Daily Column.

Page 51: From "Surrealism: Symbols of Relativity" by Andrea Martin. http://www.discovery.mala.bc.ca/web/martinar/surrealism/surrealism.htm. Reprinted by permission of Andrea Martin.

Page 52: From William Faulkner's Nobel Prize acceptance speech. © The Nobel Foundation 1950. Reprinted by permission.

Page 54: From *My Antonia* by Willa Cather. 1918.

Page 56: From Justice Byron White's opinion concurring with the court majority and Justice Harry Blackmun's opinion concurring with the court minority, U.S. Supreme Court, FURMAN v. GEORGIA, 408 U.S. 238 (1972), No. 69-5003.

<u>Dedication</u>

This book is dedicated to my brothers Casey Muehle, Eric Muehle, and Shane Weston;
to my nieces and nephews Michael, Jacob, Andrew, Alexander, Claire, Rebecca,
Emma & Nicole Muehle and Seth & Joshua Weston;
and to the students of the *Colloquium Test Prep Course for the SAT*,
Laguna Beach, California

- Lisa Muehle

Table of Contents

BASIC INFORMATION ABOUT THE SAT

SAT Format, Content & Scoring

Section of SAT	Format & Question Types	Content	Score Range
Mathematics	❏ Two 25-minute sections ❏ One 20-minute section *(Total of 70 minutes)* Mostly multiple-choice questions; some student-produced response questions.	❏ Arithmetic and Number Operations ❏ Algebra I & II ❏ Plane Geometry ❏ Coordinate Geometry ❏ Data Analysis, Statistics and Probability	M 200–800 (Lowest possible score = 200, median score = 500, "perfect" score = 800.)
Critical Reading	❏ Two 25-minute sections ❏ One 20-minute section *(Total of 70 minutes)* All multiple-choice questions.	❏ Sentence Completions ❏ Critical Reading: Reading passages ranging from 400–850 words with several accompanying questions. Short reading passages of approximately 100 words followed by one or two questions. Dual passages followed by questions about the individual passages as well as questions comparing the two passages. *Passage Subject Matter:* Natural Sciences Humanities Social Science Literary Fiction	M 200–800 (Lowest possible score = 200, median score = 500, "perfect" score = 800.)
Writing	❏ One 25-minute essay ❏ One 25-minute multiple-choice section ❏ One 10-minute multiple-choice section *(Total of 60 minutes)*	❏ Written Essay ❏ Improving Sentence Errors ❏ Improving Sentences ❏ Improving Paragraphs *Areas of Focus:* Grammar Usage Word Choice Writing Process	W 200–800 (Lowest possible score = 200, median score = 500, "perfect" score = 800.) *Two subscores are given for the writing section: a multiple-choice subscore on a scale of 20–80, and an essay subscore on a scale of 0–12. These subscores are combined and converted to the 200–800 point scale, with the essay counting for approximately 1/3 of the available Writing section points.*

Total testing time for the SAT is 3 hours and 45 minutes, which includes a 25-minute experimental section. (The experimental section is not scored.) A total of 2,400 points are available (800 points per section).

Introduction to the English Skills Areas of the SAT

The SAT format consists of three sections, two of which cover English skills. There are 2,400 points available on the SAT; 800 points are possible in each of the Critical Reading, Writing and Mathematics sections.

The Critical Reading and Writing sections on the SAT feature multiple-choice questions with five answer choices, (A) – (E). The Writing section also includes a 25-minute student written essay about a specific topic; the essay is worth approximately 1/3 of the Writing section points.

I. *Critical Reading*

Multiple-choice question types:
*   Critical reading passages followed by questions
*   Sentence completion items

Format:
70 minutes total: Two 25-minute sections and one 20-minute section.

II. *Writing*

Multiple-choice question types:
*   Sentence Correction (Usage)
*   Sentence Improvement
*   Paragraph Improvement

Written essay: Each student essay is scored by two experienced and trained high school or college instructors with respect to specific criteria. Essays are scored on a scale of 0 – 6. (A total of 12 essay points are possible from the two scorers.) The total raw essay score (0 – 12 points) is factored into the scaled Writing score in which 800 total points are possible.

Format:
60 minutes total: 25-minute essay; one 25-minute and one 10-minute multiple-choice section.

Understanding the Guessing Penalty for Wrong Answers on the SAT

The following table summarizes scoring for the SAT Critical Reading & Writing sections:

	Question is Answered Correctly	Question is Left Blank	Question is Marked with Wrong Answer
Multiple-Choice Questions with Answer Choices (A) – (E)	+ 1 point	0 points	$-\dfrac{1}{4}$ point

For student produced response questions, there is no penalty for a wrong answer. For multiple-choice questions, you will lose $\dfrac{1}{4}$ of a point for each wrong answer.

The guessing penalty actually sounds scarier than it is. If you were to randomly guess the answers to five different SAT multiple-choice questions, the odds are that you would get four questions wrong and one right (according to the basic rules of probability). These questions would be scored as follows:

$$4 \text{ questions wrong} \cdot (-\tfrac{1}{4}\text{ point}) \quad = -1 \text{ point}$$

$$\underline{1 \text{ question right} \qquad\qquad\qquad = +1 \text{ point}}$$

$$0 \text{ points}$$

So you would not have experienced any loss of points if you had guessed the answers to five questions and gotten only one right answer. This means that the "guessing penalty" is really a misnomer.

If you are able to eliminate two or even three wrong answer choices, your odds will have improved significantly. For example, if you were to guess between two answer choices on ten different questions (one of which was the correct answer), odds are that you would have answered five questions correctly (+5 points) and missed the other five questions (-1.25 points) for a net gain of 3.75 points. 3.75 points is much better than the zero points you would have had if you had left those questions blank.

Educated guessing on the SAT can help improve your score considerably. If you are stumped on a question but you can eliminate even one answer choice, you may want to guess. If you can eliminate two or more answer choices, you would be well advised to make your best educated guess. **Using process of elimination to make sound educated guesses remains the most important success strategy on the SAT.**

Suggested Study Plan

Due to the expanded content for the exam, it is best to start as early as possible in studying for the SAT. To get the most out of this book, you may wish to utilize one of the following study plans:

10-week plan: Complete one lesson per week   *5-week plan:* Complete two lessons per week

Lesson #	Approximate Time Needed	Chapter	Topic	Instructions
1: Critical Reading	1.5 hrs	1	• Introductory Material • Time Management • Scanning the Passage • Practice Critical Reading Passage with Questions	• Read & highlight text • Read practice passage and answer accompanying questions
2: Critical Reading	1 hr	2	• Clean up the Question • Locate the Answer in the Text • Eliminating Bad Answers • Main Idea • Specific Details • Author's Tone	• Read & highlight text
3: Critical Reading	1.5 hrs	3	• Paraphrasing • Inferences • Vocabulary-in-Context • Rhetorical Devices • Passage Organization • Types of Questions	• Read & highlight text
4: Critical Reading	2 hrs	4	• Practice Critical Reading Passages & Questions	• Read practice passages and answer accompanying questions • Review answer explanations
5: Critical Reading	2 hrs	5	• Sentence Completions • Practice Exercises	• Read & highlight text • Do practice exercises and review answer explanations
6: Writing	2.5 hrs	1	• Introduction • Usage Questions • Practice Exercises	• Read & highlight text • Do practice exercises and review answer explanations
7: Writing	2 hrs	2	• Improving Sentences • Practice Exercises	• Read & highlight text • Do practice exercises and review answer explanations
8: Writing	1.5 hrs	3	• Improving Paragraphs • Practice Exercises	• Read & highlight text • Do practice exercises and review answer explanations

Lesson #	Approximate Time Needed	Chapter	Topic	Instructions
9: Writing	2 hrs	4	• The Essay	• Read & highlight text
10: Writing	1 hr	4	• Writing Practice Essays	• Select two essay prompts from the selection provided on pages 179 – 180 in Writing Skills Chapter 4 • Write two 25-minute essays

Critical Reading
Chapter 1

Strategies:

1. Critical Reading Instructions & How the Questions Will Look

2. Time Management

3. Three Ways to Enhance Critical Reading Performance

4. Scan the Passage and Mark Key Terms

Practice:

Critical Reading Passage with Accompanying Questions

Tips & Strategies for Critical Reading Success
on the SAT

> ✓ **Critical Reading Strategy #1:**
>
> • **Understand the SAT's Instructions for Critical Reading Questions**
>
> • **Know How the Questions Will Look**

The directions that appear at the beginning of each Critical Reading section on the SAT indicate that questions are to be answered based upon what a passage directly states or implies, or upon information contained in the italicized introductory material.

Critical Reading selections range from 100 words to five or six paragraphs in length. Questions about each passage (as few as one, and as many as thirteen) follow.

Critical Reading questions always follow a multiple-choice format with five answer choices, (A) – (E). Here is an example:

1.   Which of the following is the best title for the passage?

(A)   Careers in Oceanography and Marine Biology

(B)   The Controversial Role of Marine Theme Parks

(C)   Marine Mammals in Captivity

(D)   Dolphin Intelligence as Evidenced in Staged Performances

(E)   Protecting Whales and Other Marine Mammals

> ✓ **Critical Reading Strategy #2:**
>
> • **Manage Your Time Carefully to Get Through All of the Questions**

There is never sufficient time to read lengthy Critical Reading passages slowly and carefully, word for word. The limited time available to read Critical Reading passages and to finish answering the accompanying questions presents a challenge to even the most literate students. Success on the Critical Reading section requires sharp concentration, shrewd assessment, and careful time management. **Study the time management suggestions that follow and try to stick to the time frames suggested when you tackle SAT Critical Reading passages.**

Successful Time Management for
Critical Reading Questions on the SAT

You should spend the majority of the time available for the Critical Reading section in answering the questions. Remember that the passage is to be used primarily as a reference tool to answer the individual questions. Spend no more than one minute reading each paragraph presented (or approximately 15 lines of text). Then spend approximately one minute answering each question; some questions will take a little less time and some a little more. You cannot, however, devote several minutes to any one particular question. If you get stuck on a question, move on! You can come back to it later, time permitting.

Description of Passage and Number of Questions	Total Time You Should Spend Reading the Passage and Answering the Questions
A five-paragraph, 71-line passage followed by 12 questions	17 minutes Reading the passage = 5 minutes Answering 12 questions = 12 minutes
A single paragraph of 100 words (approximately 10 lines) followed by 2 questions	3 minutes Reading the passage = 1 minute Answering 2 questions = 2 minutes

---

✓ Critical Reading Strategy #3:

• Employ These Three Techniques to Enhance Your Reading Comprehension

---

1. **Reduce test stress:** Develop a relaxed and composed attitude about the SAT. Students are often so obsessed about achieving high SAT scores that anxiety diminishes their reading comprehension abilities.

2. **Develop a positive attitude about the subject matter:** An unenthusiastic response to the material ("it's boring" or "it's too complicated") detracts from thoughtful evaluation of the passage.

3. **Increase concentration:** Distractibility interferes with careful interpretation of the passage and with finishing the questions in the time allowed. Stay focused!

The first two items are *emotional* and *psychological* issues and the third relates to *mental endurance*. It is important to approach Critical Reading sections with a serene and confident outlook, a mature and positive response to any subject matter that is presented, and with uninterrupted attentiveness to the text and questions. Take these steps to insure a successful approach:

- **Reduce "test anxiety"** through meditation and relaxation or breathing exercises.

- **Develop a mature and positive attitude** about the SAT's critical reading subject matter. While some of the passages' content may not be appealing or exciting to you personally, remember their purpose: to assist college admissions officials in assessing your reading comprehension abilities. SAT Critical Reading passages are not supposed to approximate what you would choose for "free reading" material. The SAT Critical Reading section is shaped to measure your ability to extract accurate meaning and draw pertinent conclusions from demanding texts.

- **Build concentration** by spending more time actively reading. There are also "brain exercises" you can learn and practice that help to "turn on" the brain, calm the mind, and improve focus.

> ✓ **Critical Reading Strategy #4:**
> • **Scan The Passage Actively**
> • **Carefully Underline or Circle Key Terms and Phrases**

There is not a lot of time to spend reading the passage, so you must do so with tremendous focus, highlighting important terms and text. Use these strategies to get the gist of the passage's content:

- ➤ **EMPLOY THE FIVE WS OF JOURNALISM: As you read, ask yourself what a reporter asks himself when he writes a newspaper article:**

Who?	Who is/are the subject(s) of the piece? Who are its main characters?
What?	What is the subject matter, theme or plot?
Where?	What is the setting for the author's discussion?
When?	When did the events in the passage occur?
Why?	Why is the author writing about this?

- ➤ **It is important to concentrate and remain very focused as you read. Ask yourself why the author decided to write this material.** Read actively. Turn the author's words into images or pictures in your mind. Predict what might come next in the text. Monitor your comprehension by asking yourself questions about the text and mentally summarizing what you have read.

- ➤ **APPROACH FOR ACADEMIC, NON-FICTION PASSAGES** (*excerpts from articles, essays, or reports drawn from natural science, social science or the humanities*): Always begin by reading the italicized introduction to the passage and then the first two or three sentences of the first paragraph. These opening lines often provide a good summary, like something the *TV Guide* would say about the passage if it were a television show. You will probably be fairly clear about the passage's purpose and main idea just from this beginning material. Now carefully read the first sentence of each paragraph. Scan the remainder of each paragraph for key words and terms.

- ➤ **APPROACH FOR EXPOSITORY NON-FICTION & FICTION PASSAGES** (*excerpts from biographies, autobiographies, personal essays, speeches, memoirs, novels or short stories*): Read the italicized introduction and then skim the passage. Focus on the main character – or, if the passage is a personal narrative, on the narrator himself. What are his circumstances? Motivations? Opinions? Aspirations? Who are the protagonist's friends or allies? Who are his enemies? As you read the passage, figure out as much as you can about what drives or challenges this main character.

- ➤ **TREAT THE PASSAGE AS IF IT WERE AN ENCYCLOPEDIA ARTICLE OR AN EXCERPT FROM AN INTERESTING BROCHURE:** Scan the text quickly to determine the passage's organizational format and its important points. Remember that the only reason the passage exists is as a reference guide for answering the questions. It is simply a source of information, nothing more.

- ➤ **MARK THE PASSAGE:** Always accentuate key terms and concepts. When you read over a Critical Reading passage, underline key words and phrases. You may also find it helpful to underline the topic sentence of each paragraph and any other sentences that make important points or summarizing statements.

The next two pages contain an example of a Critical Reading passage and accompanying questions. Read the passage and use the tips and strategies covered thus far. Additional techniques and strategies for approaching these questions will be presented in the next two Critical Reading chapters.

Following the sample passage and questions, the passage is repeated with key terms, phrases and sentences underlined.

SAMPLE CRITICAL READING PASSAGE AND QUESTIONS

Questions 1 – 12 are based on the following passage.

The following is an excerpt from a medical encyclopedia article about autoimmune disorders.

To further understand autoimmune disorders, it is helpful to understand the workings of the immune system. The purpose of the immune system is to defend the body against attack by infectious microbes (germs) and foreign
(5) objects. When the immune system attacks an invader, it is very specific – a particular immune system cell will only recognize and target one type of invader. To function properly, the immune system must not only develop this specialized knowledge of individual invaders, but it must
(10) also learn how to recognize and not destroy cells that belong to the body itself. Every cell carries protein markers on its surface that identifies it in one of two ways: what kind of cell it is (e.g. nerve cell, muscle cell, blood cell, etc.) and to whom that cell belongs. These
(15) markers are called major histocompatability complexes (MHCs). When functioning properly, cells of the immune system will not attack any other cell with markers identifying it as belonging to the body. Conversely, if the immune system cells do not recognize the cell as
(20) "self," they attach themselves to it and put out a signal that the body has been invaded, which in turn stimulates the production of substances such as antibodies that engulf and destroy the foreign particles. In the case of autoimmune disorders, the immune system cannot
(25) distinguish between "self" cells and invader cells. As a result, the same destructive operation is carried out on the body's own cells that would normally be carried out on bacteria, viruses, and other such harmful entities.

The reasons why the immune system becomes
(30) dysfunctional in this way are not well understood. However, most researchers agree that a combination of genetic, environmental, and hormonal factors play into autoimmunity. Researchers also speculate that certain mechanisms may trigger autoimmunity. First, a substance
(35) that is normally restricted to one part of the body, and therefore not usually exposed to the immune system, is released into other areas where it is attacked. Second, the immune system may mistake a component of the body for a similar foreign component. Third, cells of the body may
(40) be altered in some way, either by drugs, infection, or some other environmental factor, so that they are no longer recognizable as "self" to the immune system. Fourth, the immune system itself may be damaged, such as by a genetic mutation, and therefore cannot function
(45) properly.

1. The primary purpose of the passage is to:

(A) explain the function of the body's immune system
(B) cite the factors that contribute to autoimmunity
(C) explain the process of immune dysfunction and the possible reasons it occurs
(D) emphasize the importance of avoiding environmental disturbances that can compromise the immune system
(E) acquaint the reader with the symptoms associated with specific autoimmune disorders

2. As used in line 5, the word "invader" most nearly means:

(A) warrior
(B) enemy
(C) protein marker
(D) foreign object
(E) antibody

3. The term "histocompatability complexes" discussed in line 15 refers to:

(A) infectious microbes
(B) nerve, muscle and blood cells
(C) protein markers
(D) antibodies
(E) "self" cells

4. According to the first paragraph of the passage, autoimmune response occurs when:

(A) "self" cells are weakened by a combination of genetic, environmental and hormonal factors
(B) antibodies do not differentiate between "self" cells and invader cells and attack both
(C) the immune system is compromised by invader cells that reconfigure the body's cellular protein markers
(D) antibodies attack "self" cells only, incorrectly identifying them as foreign objects
(E) bacteria infects host cells which replicate and attack nerve, muscle and blood cells

5. A dysfunctional immune system is analogous to:

(A) an army unit ambushed by enemy forces
(B) an alarm that sounds every thirty minutes
(C) a corporate merger opposed by a group of share-holders
(D) soldiers killed by mistaken "friendly fire" from their own battalion
(E) a political dissenter who defects to another country

6. The discussion of the process of autoimmune response implies that medications or therapies successful in restoring immune tolerance to "self" cells would:

(A) generate a vaccine against autoimmunity
(B) slow the progression of autoimmune diseases
(C) enhance immune response to bacterial and viral agents
(D) improve the overall health of those with autoim-mune disorders
(E) provide a cure for those with autoimmune diseases

7. It can be inferred from the passage that the use of immunosuppressive drugs to inhibit over-active immune response would be accompanied by which of the following side effects?

(A) hormonal imbalances
(B) risk of infection
(C) rejection of transplanted organs
(D) genetic mutation
(E) a flare up of an allergic condition

8. The second paragraph of the passage serves to:

(A) identify factors and possible mechanisms that may initiate autoimmune response
(B) defend scientific efforts that have failed to cure autoimmunity
(C) address the role of drugs and infection in autoim-munity
(D) end speculation that genetic mutation is the sole cause of autoimmunity
(E) concede that scientists have not fully identified the genetic, environmental and hormonal factors involved in autoimmunity

9. In lines 33 – 45 ("Researchers also speculate... cannot function properly"), the author presents:

(A) a technical definition followed by functional analysis
(B) a general statement supported by a series of spe-cific examples
(C) a scientific theory substantiated by data analysis
(D) a quotation followed by an interpretation
(E) an assertion countered by opposing arguments

10. The word "trigger" in line 34 most nearly means:

(A) explode
(B) shoot
(C) ignite
(D) breed
(E) activate

11. According to the passage, which of the following statements are true?

I. Autoimmunity may occur when the immune system is damaged by genetic mutation.

II. Autoimmune disorders are directly inherited.

III. Autoimmune response may occur when a bodily substance moves into an area where it is not normally found, generating attack by the immune system.

(A) I only
(B) II only
(C) III only
(D) I and III
(E) I, II and III

12. Which of the following best describes the author's tone in this passage?

(A) moderate skepticism
(B) neutral objectivity
(C) veiled bewilderment
(D) marked disinterest
(E) enthusiastic admiration

Here the passage is repeated with key terms, phrases and sentences underlined:

The following is an excerpt from a medical encyclopedia article about autoimmune disorders.

To further understand autoimmune disorders, it is helpful to understand the workings of the immune system. The purpose of the immune system is to defend the body against attack by infectious microbes (germs) and foreign

(5)   objects. When the immune system attacks an invader, it is very specific – a particular immune system cell will only recognize and target one type of invader. To function properly, the immune system must not only develop this specialized knowledge of individual invaders, but it must

(10) also learn how to recognize and not destroy cells that belong to the body itself. Every cell carries protein markers on its surface that identifies it in one of two ways: what kind of cell it is (e.g. nerve cell, muscle cell, blood cell, etc.) and to whom that cell belongs. These

(15) markers are called major histocompatability complexes (MHCs). When functioning properly, cells of the immune system will not attack any other cell with markers identifying it as belonging to the body. Conversely, if the immune system cells do not recognize the cell as

(20) "self," they attach themselves to it and put out a signal that the body has been invaded, which in turn stimulates the production of substances such as antibodies that engulf and destroy the foreign particles. In the case of autoimmune disorders, the immune system cannot

(25) distinguish between "self" cells and invader cells. As a result, the same destructive operation is carried out on the body's own cells that would normally be carried out on bacteria, viruses, and other such harmful entities.

The reasons why the immune system becomes

(30) dysfunctional in this way are not well understood. However, most researchers agree that a combination of genetic, environmental, and hormonal factors play into autoimmunity. Researchers also speculate that certain mechanisms may trigger autoimmunity. First, a substance

(35) that is normally restricted to one part of the body, and therefore not usually exposed to the immune system, is released into other areas where it is attacked. Second, the immune system may mistake a component of the body for a similar foreign component. Third, cells of the body may

(40) be altered in some way, either by drugs, infection, or some other environmental factor, so that they are no longer recognizable as "self" to the immune system. Fourth, the immune system itself may be damaged, such as by a genetic mutation, and therefore cannot function

(45) properly.

If you had been taking the actual SAT I exam, you would have been able to spend no more than 15 minutes reading the previous passage about autoimmune diseases and answering the accompanying 12 questions. If it took you a bit longer, do not worry. The strategies you are about to learn will help you increase both your speed and accuracy.

CRITICAL READING

CHAPTER 1 SUMMARY

1.   **The SAT's Critical Reading section contains both Critical Reading and Sentence Completion items.**

2.   **Success on the Critical Reading section requires sharp concentration, shrewd assessment, and careful time management.**

3.   **Always begin by reading the italicized introduction to the passage and then the first two or three sentences of the first paragraph.** These opening lines often provide a good summary of the passage's main idea.

4.   Employ the five Ws of journalism as you scan a passage. **Ask yourself: *Who? What? Where? When? Why?***

5.   **When reading fictional passages, focus on the actions and motivations of the main character.**

6.   **Mark the passage as you read,** highlighting key terms and concepts.

7.   **Transitional words and phrases provide valuable cues** that help accurately anticipate and interpret upcoming text.

Critical Reading
Chapter 2

Strategies:

5. Clean Up the Question

6. Locate the Answer in the Text

7. Eliminate Bad Answer Choices

8. Identify the Main Idea

9. Answer Specific Detail Questions

10. Recognize the Author's Tone

✓ **Critical Reading Strategy #5:**

• **Clean Up the Question by Crossing Out Unnecessary Words, Underlining Key Terms, and Bracketing References to Location Within the Passage**

SAT Critical Reading questions are notorious for being unnecessarily complicated with superfluous wording and abstract, convoluted language. These questions can be made more user friendly if you do the following when you first read them:

1. ~~Cross out any unnecessary words~~
2. [Bracket line or text references]
3. Underline key terms and phrases.

Here are two examples of Critical Reading questions and how to simplify them:

> According to the third paragraph of the passage, which of the following provides the best explanation for the migratory patterns of the wild Canadian geese that the author studied?

Simplify this question as follows:

> ~~According to the~~ [third paragraph] ~~of the passage, which of the following provides the~~ best explanation for the <u>migratory patterns of the wild Canadian geese</u> ~~that the author studied?~~

Here is another example:

> The author most likely believes that the linguistic differences between the two Pre-Columbian Indian cultures discussed in lines 19 – 31 arose due to which of the following events?

Simplified version:

> ~~The author most likely believes that the~~ <u>linguistic differences between the two Pre-Columbian Indian cultures</u> ~~discussed in~~ [lines 19 – 31] arose due to ~~which of the following events~~?

✓ **Critical Reading Strategy #6:**

• **Locate the Lines of the Passage Containing the Answer to the Question and Draw a Box Around Them ("Box the Text")**

THE QUESTIONS ARE PRESENTED IN SEQUENCE WITH THE TEXT: Locating the answers to Critical Reading questions is fairly straightforward because the questions usually follow the text in order. This means that questions that refer to material in the opening paragraph will occur before questions referring to information found in the second paragraph, and questions regarding the second paragraph will be found before questions answered by the third paragraph – and so on. **Unlike Mathematics and Sentence Completion questions, Critical Reading questions will not get harder as you work in a given section – they simply follow the passage in order.**

Once you have familiarized yourself with the passage and underlined key terms and sentences, read the first question and simplify it according to Critical Reading Strategy #5. Then figure out where in the passage the answer lies. **Because the answers to the questions are usually found sequentially in the text, you should do the questions in order, starting with the first question.** Browse quickly and locate the lines you will need to answer the first question. Although it is often easier to answer the questions in the order presented, you may choose to answer thematic or global questions at the end. If you are stumped by a particular question, you can always skip it and come back to it later. After you have answered other questions about the passage, answers to some of the harder questions may become apparent.

LINE REFERENCES: Certain questions will actually provide you with "line references" telling you the vicinity of the answer. Line references read like this:

> *In lines 24 – 27 of the passage, the author indicates that the scientists first isolated the Rh factor in human blood by...*

Where would you go now? To line 21 (three lines before the cited line reference) up to line 30 (three lines after). Because you want to fully understand the referenced lines, you should read approximately three lines before and three lines after the cited text to have adequate context. The lines referenced are accurate for the most part, but the supporting context clues may be found in a few lines of text immediately preceding or immediately following the referenced material.

BOX THE TEXT: Once you have found the text lines needed to answer a particular question (either through the line references provided or through your own sleuth-like capabilities), draw a box around the material. THAT'S RIGHT – BOX THE MATERIAL! This will direct your eye to the text needed. Now systematically eliminate each answer choice by referring to the boxed text. For some questions you may need to venture outside of the boxed lines to determine the final answer.

Proceed to the next question, locate the material needed and draw another box. Repeat this process until all questions are answered.

There are certain questions that refer to the entire passage. These include certain types of main idea questions, questions about author's tone, inference questions and detail questions. In these instances, it is not possible to box the text because the text referred to is the passage in its entirety. It is best to answer these questions last – after the passage is fully digested and the other questions have been answered.

✔ Critical Reading Strategy #7:
- **Eliminate Obviously Bad Answer Choices for Each Question**

THE ANSWERS ARE RIGHT IN FRONT OF YOU: Multiple-choice test questions are like police line-ups of suspects: the possibilities are right in front of you. The correct answer is simply surrounded by four other choices. Obviously wrong answers are like hunters wearing bright orange jackets – they are easily spotted. Attractive but wrong answers are more difficult to eliminate because they are camouflaged with words or ideas that make them sound plausible. To the untrained eye, partially correct answers can seem promising.

BAD ANSWERS: Critical Reading questions usually have two or three bad answer choices that are fairly apparent. Here are some red flags for spotting bad answer choices:

1. Bad answer choices do not pertain to the question at hand, but may actually answer a different question in the set.
2. Bad answers contain absolute words including the following: *never, always, exactly, entirely, must.*
3. For detail questions, bad answers do not accurately reflect what is stated by the passage.
4. For inference questions, the conclusion drawn is either too far-fetched or is not an inference at all, but is actually something directly stated in the passage.
5. Possible primary meanings or titles are either too broad, too narrow, or entirely miss the mark.
6. Bad answers sound reasonable but actually have nothing to do with the passage's content.
7. Bad answers match your personal knowledge of the subject but are either contradicted by or not supported by the passage.

SYSTEMATICALLY EVALUATE AND ELIMINATE THE ANSWER CHOICES: After you have located the text needed to answer a particular question (and drawn a box around those lines), read answer choice (A) and refer back to the boxed text in the passage. Does the content of choice (A) have any bearing on the question? If yes, then consider choice (A) a possibility. If not, put a slash mark through the "(A)." Cross it off with finality. Do not hesitate! Now continue this process with choices (B) through (E). Refer back to the passage and determine whether or not each choice is even a viable possibility.

There will usually be two or three bad answer choices that cannot possibly work for the question. Eliminate these answers and do not give them any further consideration. This becomes a fairly effortless process with practice, as there will almost always be wrong answers that are easy to eliminate.

FINAL ANSWER: In most cases you will be able to systematically cross off all but two answer choices. Spend a few more moments referring to the text and checking for support for each remaining choice. Refine your thinking. One of the choices is the actual answer while the other just has better camouflage than the wrong answers you have already eliminated.

THE MISTAKE YOU MUST AVOID: A student crosses off (A), (C) and (D). So he has it narrowed down to (B) and (E). He says to himself, "(B) or (E), (B) or (E), (B) or (E), which is it?" He scratches his head and breaks out in a cold sweat. "(B) or (E)…Or maybe (C) is the answer…"

THAT IS THE STUDENT'S CRITICAL ERROR! If the answer was not (C) five minutes ago, it is not (C) now! Just because a student is unable to decide between (B) and (E) does not mean that (C) suddenly becomes a feasible possibility again.

Step up to the plate on these questions! Be bold! Avoid a called strike – just swing the bat! If you find yourself unable to choose between the final two answer choices, follow your intuition and pick the answer that you feel is right. Stop wavering and simply make an educated guess. Then move forward on the test without regret and do not look back. Once you have correctly narrowed the answer down to two choices, there is a fifty – fifty chance that you will be right. As you develop your skills, you will increasingly be able to detect the right answer between the two choices that remain. With practice, your final selections will turn out to be correct more often than not.

✓ **Critical Reading Strategy #8:**

• **Avoid Choices that are Too Specific or Too General for the Main Idea, Primary Purpose or Title of the Passage**

Main idea questions commonly include phrases such as these:

- *What is the main idea of the passage?*
- *The author's primary purpose is...*
- *The best title for this passage...*

They all basically mean the same thing: ***"What is this passage all about?"***

The theme, primary purpose, or main idea of the passage is not the topic of one or two of several paragraphs. It is not a subordinate idea that may occupy several lines of the text. It is definitely not a detail stated in two or three lines of the passage. And it is never a global concept that goes beyond the scope of a short passage. **The main idea is the overall essence or theme of the piece.** It is what you would write if you had to "fill in the blank" of the following sentence:

This passage mainly concerns itself with _____.

Here are examples of reasonable possibilities for the main topic of a Critical Reading passage:

- *a factual account of the women's suffrage movement from 1910 – 1920*
- *the cultural evolution of the Anasazi Indians*
- *a bittersweet recollection of the author's childhood voyages to visit his grandparents in Portugal*

Here are examples of topics that could not be the main idea of an SAT I Critical Reading passage because they are too broad for a three or four paragraph passage (these ideas would take a lengthy book or even an encyclopedia set to cover adequately):

- *Psychoanalytic theory*
- *World War II*
- *Poetry*
- *The history of the world*

Other topics fail as main ideas because they are conceptually too narrow or too trivial to warrant even a paragraph of written attention. Examples of these:

- *The third line of the second stanza of Emily Dickinson's poem, "Because I Could Not Stop for Death"*
- *How to toast a frozen waffle*
- *The late-September dietary needs of insects living near the Tropic of Capricorn*

Here are tips for identifying the main idea of the passage:

1. **Focus on the information contained in the italicized introduction to the passage and in the first two or three sentences of the first paragraph.** These lines usually provide a good synopsis of what you are about to read.

2. **Scan the text for words or phrases that occur repeatedly.** If you spot the phrase "Japanese-American filmmakers" several times in the passage, you should realize that Japanese-American filmmakers are definitely going to figure into the main idea.

3. **Read the concluding paragraph.** The last paragraph often summarizes the passage as a whole, providing a snapshot of the primary purpose of the passage.

Question 1 from the sample passage *(see page 7; black stripe on outer edge of page)* is a "main idea" question. Employ Critical Reading Strategies #5 – 7 to answer it:

-   *Clean Up the Question by Crossing Out Unnecessary Words, Underlining Key Terms and Bracketing Passage Location:*

    1. ~~The~~ <u>primary purpose</u> ~~of the passage~~ is ~~to~~:

    (A) explain the function of the body's immune system
    (B) cite the factors that contribute to autoimmunity
    (C) explain the process of immune dysfunction and the possible reasons it occurs
    (D) emphasize the importance of avoiding environmental disturbances that can compromise the immune system
    (E) acquaint the reader with the symptoms associated with specific autoimmune disorders

-   *Locate the Lines Needed and "Box the Text"*

This is a "main idea" question, so try referring to the italicized blurb and to the opening lines of each paragraph. Box the italicized blurb and the opening line of the first paragraph. The passage with important text underlined (as shown on page 9) is used for this and all other answer explanations throughout this chapter:

> *The following is an excerpt from a medical encyclopedia*
> *article about autoimmune disorders.*
>
> <u>To further understand autoimmune disorders, it is</u>

Here is the box for the opening lines of the second paragraph:

> The reasons why the immune system becomes
> 30   dysfunctional in this way are not well understood.

- ***Eliminate Bad Answer Choices***

The boxed material refers to understanding "autoimmune disorders" and to "reasons why the immune system becomes dysfunctional." We can quickly eliminate three bad answer choices. Choice (A) is a trap – it refers to the body's immune system, but not to autoimmunity. Choice (D) refers to "environmental disturbances" that are never referred to in the boxed material or in the rest of the passage. Similarly, choice (E) refers to "symptoms associated with specific autoimmune diseases" that are not even mentioned in the passage. Choices (A), (D) and (E) should be eliminated. Cross them out.

Final Answer: Choice (B) refers to only part of what the passage addresses (the information found in the second paragraph), so it is too narrow to be the main idea. Choice (C) fully summarizes what is stated in both paragraphs of the passage, so it is the best answer.

✓ Critical Reading Strategy #9:

- **To Answer Specific Detail Questions, Look for Related Explicit Statements in the Passage**

The following are examples of specific detail questions:

- *According to the second paragraph, classical music has what effect upon the brain?*

- *Spanish paleoanthropologists believe that the fossil remains of human ancestors found in northern Spain suggest which of the following?*

- *In lines 13 – 38 of the passage, the author indicates that the essential difference between continental crust and oceanic crust is:*

- *The narrator's grandparents moved to Arcadia before the war broke out because:*

CAREFULLY FIND AND CONFIRM SPECIFIC DETAILS: Specific detail questions require that you pay careful attention to the text, to what exactly the question is asking, and to the content of the answer choices. Use the following techniques to answer detail questions:

1. **Make sure that you have carefully boxed the text** needed to answer the question.

2. **Identify any key words or terms the answer choices contain.** Scan the boxed text and circle these key words.

3. **Read each answer choice very carefully and compare it with the boxed text.** Does the answer choice state, re-state, summarize or clarify any of the material in the boxed text? If so, does it answer the question that is being asked?

4. **Eliminate answer choices that contain key terms or words that are not found in the boxed material.** If an answer choice refers to "early French Impressionism" and "early French Impressionism" is not even mentioned in the boxed text, you can probably eliminate the answer choice as an option.

5. **Do not rely on your own understanding of the subject to answer the questions.** On specific detail questions, students are particularly susceptible to drawing upon their own knowledge of the subject rather than utilizing the passage as the only source that should be used to answer the questions. Remember that these questions are not about what you have learned in school or in life; the questions are to be answered strictly by the contents of the passage. Suppose you come across a Critical Reading passage about the breeding habits of iguanas and other related reptiles; you are delighted because you have a pet iguana and are an expert on the subject. Do not let your wealth of knowledge about iguanas become a factual source for answering the questions! Consult the passage to find the answers. The answers to the questions must be found in the passage, not in your head.

Question 3 from the sample passage is a "specific detail" question *(see page 7; black stripe on outer edge of page)*. We will utilize Critical Reading Strategies #5 – #7 once again to find the answer:

- ***Clean Up the Question by Crossing Out Unnecessary Words, Underlining Key Terms and Bracketing Passage Location:***

    3.   ~~The term~~ "<u>histocompatability complexes</u>" ~~discussed in~~ [line 15] refers to:

    (A)   infectious microbes
    (B)   nerve, muscle and blood cells
    (C)   protein markers
    (D)   antibodies
    (E)   "self" cells

- ***Locate the Lines Needed and "Box the Text"***

The question says that the term "histocompatibility complexes" is found in line 15. The text to box in this case includes the sentence containing the term as well as the preceding sentence, which foregrounds the term:

> <u>belong to the body itself</u>. Every cell carries <u>protein</u>
> <u>markers</u> on its surface that identifies it in one of two
> ways: what kind of cell it is (e.g. nerve cell, muscle cell,
> blood cell, etc.) and to whom that cell belongs. These
> 15   markers are called <u>major histocompatability complexes</u>

- ***Eliminate Bad Answer Choices***

None of the boxed material refers to the terms found in choices (A) or (D), so they can be eliminated. The phrase "these markers are called major histocompatibility complexes" indicates that rather than being actual cells themselves, the histocompatibility complexes serve as cellular markers. Thus choices (B) and (E) can also be eliminated, and the answer is (C).

Question 4 from the sample passage *(see page 7; black stripe on outer edge of page)* is another "specific detail" question:

- ***Clean Up the Question by Crossing Out Unnecessary Words, Underlining Key Terms and Bracketing Passage Location:***

  4.   ~~According to the~~ [first paragraph] ~~of the passage~~, <u>autoimmune response</u> occurs when:

  (A)   "self" cells are weakened by a combination of genetic, environmental and hormonal factors

  (B)   antibodies do not differentiate between "self" cells and invader cells and attack both

  (C)   the immune system is compromised by invader cells that reconfigure the body's cellular protein markers

  (D)   antibodies attack "self" cells only, incorrectly identifying them as foreign objects

  (E)   bacteria infects host cells which replicate and attack nerve, muscle and blood cells

- ***Locate the Lines Needed and "Box the Text"***

The question indicates that the text needed is found in the first paragraph. This means that it probably comes fairly near, and most probably immediately after, the material needed for the last question, which was found in lines 10 – 20. Lines 19 – 28 discuss "mistaken immune response":

> identifying it as belonging to the body. <u>Conversely,
> if the immune system cells do not recognize the cell as</u>
> 20   <u>"self," they attach themselves to it and put out a signal
> that the body has been invaded,</u> which in turn stimulates
> the production of substances such as antibodies that
> engulf and destroy the foreign particles. <u>In the case of
> autoimmune disorders, the immune system cannot</u>
> 25   <u>distinguish between "self" cells and invader cells.
> As a result, the same destructive operation is carried out
> on the body's own cells that would normally be carried
> out on bacteria, viruses, and other such harmful entities.</u>

- ***Eliminate Bad Answer Choices***

Answer choices (A), (C), and (E) can be eliminated from consideration. Choice (A) refers to genetic, environmental and hormonal factors, choice (C) refers to reconfiguring the body's cellular protein, and choice (E) refers to attack of nerve, muscle and blood cells; none of these terms are discussed in the boxed text.

Final Answer: Choices (B) and (D) remain. According to the boxed text (lines 24 – 25), the mistaken immune process occurs when antibodies "cannot distinguish between 'self' cells and invader cells." This is directly restated in answer choice (B), which is the correct answer.

Triple True/False Questions

One type of specific detail question is the "triple true/false" question in which three statements are presented. Each statement is either true (supported by the passage) or false (not supported by or perhaps even contradicted by the passage). The answer choices present various combinations of the statements as true.

These questions can be time consuming, as you must evaluate each of the three statements. The best approach is to start with the easiest statement (often the shortest) to verify within the text. For example, you may be able to quickly determine that statement II is false. This would mean that any answer choices containing statement II could be eliminated.

Question 11 from the sample passage *(see page 8; black stripe on outer edge of page)* is a "triple true/false" question:

- *Clean Up the Question by Crossing Out Unnecessary Words, Underlining Key Terms and Bracketing Passage Location:*

    11. ~~According to the passage~~, which ~~of the following~~ statements are true?

    I.   Autoimmunity may occur when the immune system is damaged by genetic mutation.

    II. Autoimmune disorders are directly inherited.

    III. Autoimmune response may occur when a bodily substance moves into an area where it is not normally found, generating attack by the immune system.

    (A) I only
    (B) II only
    (C) III only
    (D) I and III
    (E) I, II and III

- *Locate the Lines Needed and "Box the Text"*

Because this is a triple true/false question in which certain statements are true and others may be false, one or more of the statements will appear as points that are made somewhere in the passage. It can be very difficult to "box the text" for this question type. Instead, it makes more sense to scan for the key words in each answer choice and take note of the sentences containing confirmation of those answer choices that are supported by the passage. The following lines are excerpted from the second paragraph of the passage; the emboldened sentences confirm statements (III) and (I) respectively:

> mechanisms may trigger autoimmunity. **First, a substance**
> 35   **that is normally restricted to one part of the body, and**
> **therefore not usually exposed to the immune system, is**
> **released into other areas where it is attacked.** Second, the
> immune system may mistake a component of the body for
> a similar foreign component. Third, cells of the body may

40   be altered in some way, either by drugs, infection, or
       some other environmental factor, so that they are no
       longer recognizable as "self" to the immune system.
       **Fourth, the immune system itself may be damaged, such
       as by a genetic mutation, and therefore cannot function**
45   **properly.**

- *Eliminate Bad Answer Choices*

Statements I and III are both true. Further examination of the text reveals that statement II is not supported by the passage. The second paragraph indicates that "genetic factors" and "genetic mutation" may contribute to autoimmunity, but the passage does not state that the condition is "directly inherited." The correct answer is (D).

Except/Least/Not Questions

Certain specific detail questions carry the "triple true/false" concept one step further and ask you to identify the single answer choice that contains incorrect information. These questions may be worded as follows:

- *"According to the passage, all of the following are true EXCEPT..."*
- *"Which of the following does NOT support the author's argument?"*
- *"With which of the following statements would the author be LEAST likely to agree?"*

Many careless errors are made in answering these questions. **You must remember that you are looking for the one answer choice that is <u>wrong</u>.** The best way to proceed is by process of elimination. Systematically identify and eliminate answer choices that are true. There will be one choice left that cannot be corroborated by the passage. That will be the answer!

✓ Critical Reading Strategy #10:

- **Identifying the Author's Tone**

Whether or not an author intends it, every piece of his writing expresses a certain tone. An author bears a certain attitude toward his topic and his audience that is revealed by his work. An author's tone may be objective (detached, unbiased, or neutral) or subjective (impassioned, biased, or argumentative). Questions about tone may be worded as follows:

- *"Which of the following best expresses the author's tone?"*
- *"The author's presentation of his subject..."*
- *"The author's point of view in this passage..."*
- *"The author most likely thinks his audience..."*

When you first skim the passage, ask yourself whether the author is neutral about his subject or whether he expresses an opinion or feelings about it. Is the author's presentation objective or subjective? Critical or sympathetic? Admiring or disdainful?

Critical and literary essays are intended to be informative, and they usually employ a serious and objective tone. In these works, the author usually supports his claim with supporting evidence rather than stating his feelings or opinions. In writing that is strictly informational, authors do not allow their biases to show. Phrases that describe a neutral or objective tone include "scientific detachment," "objective neutrality," and "unbiased objectivity."

In subjective works, the author's choice of language can be very revealing with respect to tone. The selection of a single word or phrase can affect the tone of an entire paragraph or essay. The author's perspective of certain events also influences the tone. Is the excerpt wry, dry, objective, cynical, nostalgic, hopeful? Try to pick up on some key adjectives and adverbs, descriptive words that communicate tone. Ask yourself this: what does the author have strong feelings about? Then pinpoint the nature of these emotions.

Question 12 from the sample passage *(see page 8; black stripe on outer edge of page)* is a question about the author's tone.

- *Clean Up the Question by Crossing Out Unnecessary Words, Underlining Key Terms and Bracketing Passage Location:*

  12. Which ~~of the following best~~ describes the <u>author's tone</u> ~~in this passage~~?

  (A) moderate skepticism
  (B) neutral objectivity
  (C) veiled bewilderment
  (D) marked disinterest
  (E) enthusiastic admiration

- *Locate the Lines Needed and "Box the Text"*

This cannot be done because this is a question about tone that concerns the passage as a whole.

- *Eliminate Bad Answer Choices*

The passage about autoimmunity appears to have been taken from a medical reference book of some type. The tone of this article is one of scientific detachment. Four unsuitable answers are (A), (C), (D) and (E). Choice (B) is the only answer that accurately describes the tone of this sort of article.

CRITICAL READING

CHAPTER 2 SUMMARY

1. **Clean up Critical Reading questions** to reduce "fog content." Cross out unnecessary words, underline key terms, and bracket references to location within the passage.

2. Locating the answers to Critical Reading questions is fairly straightforward because **the questions usually follow the text in order.**

3.   **Most Critical Reading questions usually have two or three bad answer choices** that are fairly obvious and can be eliminated.

4.   **The main idea, primary purpose, or title of the passage must suit its content.** It should not be stated too specifically or too generally.

5.   **Carefully find and confirm specific details.** Specific detail questions require that you pay careful attention to the text, to what exactly the question is asking, and to the content of each answer choice.

6.   **Academic non-fiction passages found on the SAT I usually have a neutral, objective tone.** The tone of fictional and narrative non-fiction passages is conveyed by the author's use of descriptive language and by the feelings and perspective he has about his subject or characters.

Critical Reading
Chapter 3

Strategies:

11. Paraphrasing

12. Drawing Inferences

13. Vocabulary-in-Context Questions

14. Literary Techniques & Rhetorical Devices

15. Passage Organization (Structural Forms & Techniques)

16. Dual Passages

17. Types of Critical Reading Passages found on the SAT I

✓ **Critical Reading Strategy #11:**

• **Practice Paraphrasing**

Some questions on the SAT I ask you to summarize portions of the text. The synopsis stated in the correct answer choice must be an accurate re-statement that addresses key points. Consider the following passage from the novel *Wuthering Heights*:

> *But Mr. Heathcliff forms a singular contrast to his abode and style of living. He is a dark-skinned gypsy in aspect, in dress and manners a gentleman: that is, as much a gentleman as many a country squire: rather slovenly, perhaps, yet not looking amiss with his negligence, because he has an erect and handsome figure; and rather morose. Possibly some people might suspect him of a degree of under-bred pride; I have a sympathetic chord within that tells me it is nothing of the sort: I know, by instinct, his reserve springs from an aversion to showy displays of feeling – to manifestations of mutual kindliness. He'll love and hate equally under cover, and esteem it a species of impertinence to be loved or hated again.*

A good way to paraphrase is to pick up key phrases right from the text. The "boiling down" process can often simply consist of lifting out key ingredients:

His appearance is that of: *a slightly slovenly gentleman.*
His manner is: *reserved, with an "aversion to showy displays of feeling."*

Try paraphrasing yourself. Read a newspaper article and try to summarize it in three or five sentences. Try to get to the heart of everything you read. Discard minor details and re-state the main idea. Learn to say it in a sentence.

Question 8 from the sample passage *(see page 8; black stripe on outer edge of page)* is a paraphrasing question:

• *Clean Up the Question by Crossing Out Unnecessary Words, Underlining Key Terms and Bracketing Passage Location:*

8.   The [second paragraph] ~~of the passage~~ serves to:

(A)   identify factors and possible mechanisms that may initiate autoimmune response

(B)   defend scientific efforts that have failed to cure autoimmunity

(C)   address the role of drugs and infection in autoimmunity

(D)   end speculation that genetic mutation is the sole cause of autoimmunity

(E)   concede that scientists have not fully identified the genetic, environmental and hormonal factors involved in autoimmunity

- *Locate the Lines Needed and "Box the Text"*

What the question is asking for is a summary, or paraphrase, of the second paragraph, so "box" the paragraph in its entirety:

> The reasons why the immune system becomes
> 30 dysfunctional in this way are not well understood.
> <u>However, most researchers agree that a combination of</u>
> <u>genetic, environmental, and hormonal factors play into</u>
> <u>autoimmunity. Researchers also speculate that certain</u>
> <u>mechanisms may trigger autoimmunity.</u> First, a substance
> 35 that is normally restricted to one part of the body, and
> therefore not usually exposed to the immune system, is
> released into other areas where it is attacked. Second, the
> immune system may mistake a component of the body for
> a similar foreign component. Third, cells of the body may
> 40 be altered in some way, either by drugs, infection, or
> some other environmental factor, so that they are no
> longer recognizable as "self" to the immune system.
> Fourth, the immune system itself may be damaged, such
> as by a genetic mutation, and therefore cannot function
> 45 properly.

- *Eliminate Bad Answer Choices*

The opening lines of the boxed paragraph indicate that the reasons for immune dysfunction are not well understood, but that genetic, environmental and hormonal factors may be involved. The paragraph continues with a list of possible triggers of autoimmunity. Three bad answer choices are apparent. Choice (B) can be eliminated because the paragraph does not address any efforts to cure autoimmunity. Choice (C) is incorrect because drugs and infection are mentioned as one possible contributor to autoimmunity, but the whole of the paragraph does not address this issue. Likewise, answer choice (D) refers to genetic mutation as a cause of autoimmunity, but the paragraph addresses other matters as well.

Final Answer: The correct paraphrase must summarize the paragraph's main purpose. Choice (E) refers to the opening lines of the paragraph indicating that scientists have not fully identified the "genetic, environmental and hormonal factors" that contribute to autoimmunity, but this is not the paragraph's key point. Choice (A) provides the best summary or paraphrase, which is to "identify factors and possible mechanisms that may initiate autoimmune response."

✓ Critical Reading Strategy #12:
- ### Approaching Inference Questions, or The Fine Art of Drawing Conclusions

---

Inference questions require you to draw a conclusion based on what is stated in the passage. To make correct inferences you must read between the lines and form valid interpretations based on what is explicitly stated in the text.

Here is an example of a Critical Reading selection followed by an inference question:

> *Biologists visited a Nordic region where all of the dogs have a light-blue tint to their fur. The scientists have theorized that over the generations, the light-blue coloring has developed because blue-tipped fur allows the dogs to blend in with the blue-green needles of local spruce trees.*

It can be inferred that dogs in the Nordic region are blue because:

(A)   They are very cold.

(B)   Somehow their food got contaminated with blue food coloring.

(C)   They blend in with the blue-green trees.

(D)   The evolutionary process has favored the development of blue dogs because they are the most fit to survive in their native habitat.

(E)   Dogs in the Nordic region are not blue. Dogs in the Nordic region are red. Everyone knows that.

Inference questions require you to draw a conclusion based on what is stated in the passage. To make correct inferences you must read between the lines and form valid interpretations. Inference questions are worded as follows:

- *"The author **implies** which of the following about the blue dogs of the Nordic region..."*

- *"The reader can **infer** which of the following about the Nordic region's blue dogs..."*

- *"Based on the information provided about the blue dogs of the Nordic region, one can **conclude**..."*

- *"The passage **suggests** which of the following about the Nordic region's blue dogs..."*

THERE ARE TWO THINGS YOU SHOULD KNOW ABOUT INFERENCE QUESTIONS:

1.   What one can infer is **not** directly stated in the passage. It is *suggested*, but not *directly stated*, in the passage.

2.   The conclusion you draw must be based entirely upon what is stated in the passage. This means your answer must make a reasonable, deductive leap. You need to find the answer choice that contains the most logical conclusion to be drawn based on what is actually stated in the text. That means one reasonable leap, not three or four misdirected leaps. The conclusion drawn cannot be farfetched.

For example, if you see a rainbow, you can reasonably infer that it has recently rained. You could not reasonably conclude, however, that the rain clouds have moved northeast and are forming a hurricane.

For the short passage above regarding the blue dogs in the Nordic region, examine each answer choice in the context of what is expected for correctly drawn inferences:

(A)   They are very cold. *(THIS IS PROBABLY TRUE, BUT IT IS NOT A STATEMENT SUPPORTED BY THE PASSAGE.)*

(B)   Somehow their food got contaminated with blue food coloring. *(THIS INFERENCE IS NOT SUPPORTED BY THE PASSAGE.)*

(C)   They blend in with the blue-green trees. *(THIS IS DIRECTLY STATED BY THE PASSAGE; THIS IS THE CHOICE THAT THE TEST WRITERS THINK YOU MIGHT FALL FOR. NOTICE HOW THIS TEMPTING CHOICE IS PLACED IN (C) – JUST BEFORE THE ANSWER, WHICH IS ACTUALLY IN CHOICE (D). REMEMBER TO ALWAYS CHECK EVERY ANSWER CHOICE!)*

(D)   The evolutionary process has favored the development of blue dogs because they are the most fit to survive in their native habitat. *(HERE IS THE ANSWER; THIS IS A REASONABLE CONCLUSION THAT CAN BE DRAWN BASED ON INFORMATION STATED IN THE PASSAGE.)*

(E)   Dogs in the Nordic region are not blue. Dogs in the Nordic region are red. Everyone knows that. *(RED DOGS APPARENTLY LIVE IN A COMPLETELY DIFFERENT PART OF THE NORDIC REGION.)*

Question 6 from the sample passage *(see page 8; black stripe on outer edge of page)* is an inference question:

- ***Clean Up the Question by Crossing Out Unnecessary Words, Underlining Key Terms and Bracketing Passage Location:***

    6.   [The discussion of the process of autoimmune response] <u>implies</u> that <u>medications</u> or therapies <u>successful in restoring immune tolerance</u> to "self" cells would:

    (A)   generate a vaccine against autoimmunity
    (B)   slow the progression of autoimmune diseases
    (C)   enhance immune response to bacterial and viral agents
    (D)   improve the overall health of those with autoimmune disorders
    (E)   provide a cure for those with autoimmune diseases

- ***Locate the Lines Needed and "Box the Text"***

    The "discussion of the process of autoimmune response" was previously referenced for question 4. The end of the first paragraph refers to the attack of "self" cells:

> engulf and destroy the foreign particles. <u>In the case of autoimmune disorders, the immune system cannot</u>
> 25   <u>distinguish between "self" cells and invader cells.</u>
> <u>As a result, the same destructive operation is carried out on the body's own cells that would normally be carried out on bacteria, viruses, and other such harmful entities.</u>

- ***Eliminate Bad Answer Choices***

The text directly states that "the immune system cannot distinguish between 'self' cells and invader cells." This implies that a healthy immune system does make such a distinction. The question asks what the restoration of immune tolerance to "self" cells would signify. It would mean that the immune system would become tolerant again of the body's own cells and not attack them, resulting in a reversal of the autoimmune process and a return to a healthy immune system. There are three answer choices that, given careful thought, can be ruled out. Choice (A) can be eliminated because restorative "medications or therapies" would be administered as a treatment following the onset of disease; these would neither constitute nor "generate" a vaccine administered beforehand to prevent autoimmune disorders from manifesting in the first place. Choice (B) is incorrect because a properly functioning immune system would prohibit the very process of autoimmunity, not just slow disease progression. Choice (C) is wrong because there is no basis for connecting a halted immune system assault upon "self" cells with a more vigorous immune response against germs.

Final Answer: Two possible inferences remain. Choice (D) could be inferred in a general sense, as the restoration of immune tolerance to "self" cells would counteract autoimmunity, obviously resulting in improved health. But choice (E) is the natural conclusion that can be drawn because "medications or therapies successful in restoring immune tolerance to 'self' cells" would indeed re-establish a completely healthy immune system, the equivalent of "a cure for those with autoimmune disease." The answer is (E).

Question 7 from the sample passage *(see page 8; black stripe on outer edge of page)* is another inference question:

- ***Clean Up the Question by Crossing Out Unnecessary Words, Underlining Key Terms and Bracketing Passage Location:***

    7.   ~~It can be~~ inferred ~~from the passage that the use of immunosuppressive~~ drugs to inhibit over-active immune response would be accompanied by which ~~of the following~~ unwanted side effects?

    (A)   hormonal imbalances
    (B)   risk of infection
    (C)   rejection of transplanted organs
    (D)   genetic mutation
    (E)   a flare up of an allergic condition

- ***Locate the Lines Needed and "Box the Text"***

Drugs used to address "over-active immune response" would probably interfere with all immune response processes, healthy and unhealthy alike. The "unwanted side effect," therefore, would be the drug's undesired interference with healthy immune response. The text we should box should address proper immune response. Discussion of normal immune response is found in two sections of the first paragraph:

> The purpose of the immune system is to defend the body
> against attack by infectious microbes (germs) and foreign
> 5   objects. When the immune system attacks an invader, it is

> 26   As a result, the same destructive operation is carried out
>   on the body's own cells that would normally be carried
>   out on bacteria, viruses, and other such harmful entities.

- ***Eliminate Bad Answer Choices***

The text indicates that the role of the immune system is to attack "infectious microbes (germs) and foreign objects" and "bacteria, viruses and other such harmful entities." The immune system's purpose is obviously to thwart these "invader" cells that make the body ill. Choices (A), (C), and (D) are clearly incorrect because they have nothing to do with illness or disease caused by bacteria or infectious microbes.

Final Answer: The inference drawn must be a direct result of bacterial or microbial activity. Choice (E), "a flare up of an allergic condition," is not directly caused by germs. But choice (B), the "risk of infection," would occur if bacteria or infectious microbes were left unchecked. The answer is (B).

✓ **Critical Reading Strategy #13:**

- **The Angle on Vocabulary-in-Context Questions**

Vocabulary-in-Context questions are just like Sentence Completion questions with a twist. *Example:*

In the sentence above, the word "twist" means:

(A)   turn
(B)   bend
(C)   curve
(D)   rotate
(E)   embellishment

You should immediately see that answer choices (A) – (D) are all PRIMARY meanings of the word "twist." On Vocabulary-in-Context questions the writers of the SAT are only occasionally interested in the primary meaning of the word, so you can usually rule those choices out. The right answer is (E), "embellishment." A *twist* can be an embellishment (adornment, enhancement, garnishment).

To answer these questions successfully, find the word in the sentence, cover it with your finger, and choose the word from the answer choices that best fits in its place. Substitute each choice, one at a time, and eliminate those that do not work.

THE ANSWER CHOICES WILL CONTAIN SYNONYMS FOR VARIOUS MEANINGS OF THE WORD. The key to success is reading the entire sentence in which the word appears. Do not just look at the answer choices and select a synonym for the word in question. That is where you will derail every time because the SAT writers make sure that several of the answer choices can be synonyms for the word in *some* context – just not in the given one.

Often these questions are intended to sidetrack you with the primary meanings of words when the answer really involves a secondary definition. *Example:*

The Sea World attendant plans to train the seals to do the backstroke.

In the sentence above, the word "train" means:

(A)   locomotive (means "train")
(B)   wedding dress attachment (means "train")
(C)   teach (means "train")
(D)   breed
(E)   feed

The first two trains are not on the right track. Take those trains and you missed the one you needed, which was choice (C). Notice that it is also possible to breed seals and feed seals, something a Sea World attendant might also do. If you do not read the sentence carefully, you could pick (D) or (E).

Question 2 from the sample passage *(see page 7 black stripe on outer edge of page)* is a Vocabulary-in-Context question:

- **Clean Up the Question by Crossing Out Unnecessary Words, Underlining Key Terms and Bracketing Passage Location:**

  2.   ~~As used in~~ [line 5], ~~the word~~ "invader" ~~most nearly~~ means:

(A)   warrior
(B)   enemy
(C)   protein marker
(D)   foreign object
(E)   antibody

- **Locate the Lines Needed and "Box the Text"**

Box the lines containing the sentence with the word "invader" (line 5), and, for context, the sentence immediately before that sentence. Be sure to box or circle the word "invader" in line 5:

> The purpose of the immune system is to defend the body against attack by infectious microbes (germs) and foreign
> 5   objects. When the immune system attacks an invader , it is
> very specific – a particular immune system cell will only recognize and target one type of invader. To function

- ***Eliminate Bad Answer Choices***

Choices (A) and (B) are probably incorrect because "warrior" and "enemy" are both synonyms for the primary meaning of "invader."

Final Answer: The word "invader" is used in line 5 to refer back to the "infectious microbes (germs) and foreign objects" identified in the previous sentence as the immune system's adversaries. The answer is (D).

Question 10 from the sample passage *(see page 8; black stripe on outer edge of page)* is another Vocabulary-in-Context question:

- ***Clean Up the Question by Crossing Out Unnecessary Words, Underlining Key Terms and Bracketing Passage Location:***

    10.   ~~The word~~ "trigger" in [line 34] ~~most nearly~~ means:

    (A)   explode
    (B)   shoot
    (C)   ignite
    (D)   breed
    (E)   activate

- ***Locate the Lines Needed and "Box the Text"***

Examine the sentence in which the word "trigger" appears:

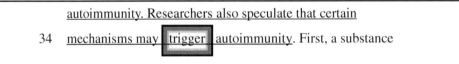

autoimmunity. Researchers also speculate that certain

34   mechanisms may trigger autoimmunity. First, a substance

- ***Eliminate Bad Answer Choices***

(A), (B), and (C) are poor choices because "explode," "shoot," and "ignite" are all words reminiscent of the primary meaning of the word "trigger" or of firearms associated with the word "trigger."

Final Answer: Of the two remaining choices, (D) does not make sense in the sentence:

Researchers also speculate that certain mechanisms may breed autoimmunity.

Autoimmunity is not something that is "bred." It is, however, something that is "activated":

Researchers also speculate that certain mechanisms may activate autoimmunity.

This sounds right, which is a good sign. The answers to Vocabulary-in-Context questions should sound correct to the human ear. The answer is (E).

✓ **Critical Reading Strategy #14:**
• **Become Familiar with Literary Techniques and Rhetorical Devices Used by Authors in SAT Critical Reading Passages**

The SAT's Critical Reading questions require students to be familiar with literary techniques and rhetorical devices commonly encountered in a high school literature course. You will not have to provide definitions for these terms, but you should have a working knowledge of significant literary terms. The following charts should help:

Figurative Language

RHETORICAL DEVICE	DEFINITION	EXAMPLES
Metaphor	Comparison of two different things without using words such as "like" or "as."	• "Juliet is the sun." – Shakespeare, *Romeo and Juliet* • He was a wolf in sheep's clothing.
Simile	Comparison of two different things using "like" or "as."	• "My love is like a red, red rose." – Robert Burns • The quarterback was as cool as a cucumber.
Personification	Attributes human characteristics to an animal, object or idea.	• The old train coughed as it sputtered up the hill. • The flower nodded in the mid-day sun.
Allusion	Reference to someone or something from past literature or history. The Bible, Shakespeare and Greek & Roman mythology are all rich sources for allusions.	• Renovating the downtown area will be a Herculean task. • The quadruplets' mother has the patience of Job.
Hyperbole	Exaggerated language used for emphasis or comic effect.	"An hundred years should go to praise Thine eyes and on thy forehead gaze; Two hundred to adore each breast; But thirty thousand to the rest…" – Andrew Marvell, *To His Coy Mistress*

Other Rhetorical Devices

RHETORICAL DEVICE	DEFINITION	EXAMPLES
Analogy	A comparison in which the <u>relationship</u> involved in one situation, process or set of objects or ideas is parallel to the <u>relationship</u> involved in another situation, process, or set of objects or ideas. Often one part of the analogy is more familiar and serves to clarify the other less familiar or more abstract part.	"One Hundred and Twenty-fifth Street was to Harlem what the Mississippi was to the South, a long traveling river always going somewhere, carrying something." – Maya Angelou, *Heart of a Woman*
Antithesis	The juxtaposition (joining together) of opposite ideas to sharpen their contrast.	"To err is human; to forgive, divine." – Alexander Pope
Rhetorical Question	A question posed to emphasize an important fact or to commence development of a significant point.	"Shall I compare thee to a summer's day?" – William Shakespeare, *18th Sonnet*
Irony	A contradiction between appearance or apparent meaning and reality or real meaning. A discrepancy between what is expected to happen and what actually happens (usually a turn of events, a twist, or an unexpected surprise).	"An old man turned ninety-eight He won the lottery and died the next day It's a black fly in your Chardonnay It's a death row pardon two minutes too late." – Alanis Morissette, *Ironic*
Paradox	A self-contradictory statement that conveys truthful meaning.	• "Cowards die many times before their deaths." – Shakespeare, *Julius Caesar* • Sometimes silence speaks the loudest.
Oxymoron	A two-word paradox.	• "Why then, O brawling love! O loving hate! O heavy lightness, serious vanity; Misshapen chaos of well-seeming forms! Feather of lead, bright smoke, cold fire, sick health!" – William Shakespeare, *Romeo and Juliet* • jumbo shrimp, deafening silence, original copy
Euphemism	An agreeable or inoffensive word or phrase substituted for an expression that is blunt or unpleasant.	• "pre-owned vehicles" is a phrase popular among used car salesmen • "collateral damage" is a military term for civilians killed during combat • "at variance with the facts" refers to a lie
Understatement	The opposite of hyperbole; stated with restraint, which actually serves to add emphasis.	"To lose one parent, Mr. Worthing, may be regarded as a misfortune; to lose both looks like carelessness." – Oscar Wilde, *The Importance of Being Earnest*

RHETORICAL DEVICE	DEFINITION	EXAMPLES
Parody	Exaggerated, comic imitation of a person, event or piece of literature.	• In *Don Quixote*, Cervantes creates a parody of medieval romance • In "The Nun's Priest Tale" from the *Canterbury Tales*, Chaucer parodies the fall of Troy

Question 5 from the sample passage *(see page 8; black stripe on outer edge of page)* refers to a rhetorical device:

- ***Clean Up the Question by Crossing Out Unnecessary Words, Underlining Key Terms and Bracketing Passage Location:***

    5.   A dysfunctional immune system is analogous to:

    (A)   an army unit ambushed by enemy forces
    (B)   an alarm that sounds every thirty minutes
    (C)   a corporate merger opposed by a group of shareholders
    (D)   soldiers killed by mistaken "friendly fire" from their own battalion
    (E)   a political dissenter who defects to another country

- ***Locate the Lines Needed and "Box the Text"***

The location for the text needed should be very near the text referenced for questions 4 and 6. The question refers to the process of the dysfunctional immune system, which is described in the last portion of the first paragraph, beginning with line 18:

>   identifying it as belonging to the body. Conversely,
>   if the immune system cells do not recognize the cell as
> 20   "self," they attach themselves to it and put out a signal
>   that the body has been invaded, which in turn stimulates
>   the production of substances such as antibodies that
>   engulf and destroy the foreign particles. In the case of
>   autoimmune disorders, the immune system cannot
> 25   distinguish between "self" cells and invader cells.
>   As a result, the same destructive operation is carried out
>   on the body's own cells that would normally be carried
>   out on bacteria, viruses, and other such harmful entities.

- ***Eliminate Bad Answer Choices***

The question asks which answer choice presents a scenario that is "analogous" to a dysfunctional immune system. The correct answer choice will contain an analogy to this process. In the literal sense, a dysfunctional immune system attacks its body's own cells. Choices (B) and (E) can be discarded because neither mentions any sort of assault. Choice (C) refers to a conflict, but it does not involve a physical attack, so choice (C) can also be eliminated.

Final Answer: The primary difference between the remaining choices (A) and (D) is the source of the attack. In Choice (A), an opposing force is the source of the assault. In Choice (D), the attack mistakenly comes from the same side. Choice (D) is the best analogy because a dysfunctional immune system attacks its own "self" cells.

✓ **Critical Reading Strategy #15:**

• **Recognize a Paragraph's or Passage's Organizational Pattern**

Some Critical Reading questions for non-fiction passages ask you to identify the author's organizational scheme, technique or structural form. It is important to be familiar with the literary "blueprints," the organizing principles and structural formats that authors commonly utilize. The following are some of the organizational schemes found on SAT Critical Reading passages:

Organizational Pattern	Starts with:	Followed by:	Example
General to Specific • **Assertion Supported by Evidence** • **Thesis Followed by Factual References** • **Argument Substantiated by Specific Data** • **General Statement Supported by Specific Examples**	A statement that asserts a position or makes a claim	Concrete supporting statements (factual references, historical evidence, illustrative examples, statistics, reports, quotations of authorities, and personal testimony)	The Declaration of Independence's assertion that the "history of the present King of Great Britain is a history of repeated injuries and usurpations," followed by specific examples of his "absolute Tyranny over these States"
Specific to General • **Specific Instances Followed by a Generalization** • **Observations Leading to a Supposition** • **Presentation of Data Concluded by a Theory**	A series of specific instances, observations, examples and data is presented and examined	A generalization, a supposition, a conclusion, or a theory	A presentation outlining various UFO sightings followed by the theory that extraterrestrials have visited the earth
Philosophical Reasoning/Logical Deduction *(Traditional Aristotelian logic is used to advance the author's argument)*	An argument developed via deductive reasoning (a series of syllogisms, or "if…then" statements)	A valid concluding statement or deduction	The following famous syllogism illustrates Aristotelian logic: 1. Socrates is a man. 2. All men are mortal. 3. Therefore, Socrates is mortal.

Organizational Pattern	Starts with:	Followed by:	Example
Functional Analysis	An object or process is broken down into its component parts	Each part is systematically examined and evaluated with respect to its function as well as to its contribution to the whole entity	An article that details how a clock works
Cause and Effect *(The causal argument is that one event or a sequence of events necessarily causes or results in a certain outcome or leads to specific consequences.)*	Identification of a causal factor or factors	Acknowledgement of the inevitable results or consequences	A report regarding the causes and effects of Mississippi River spring flooding
Time Sequence	A series of events is presented in chronological order		An article outlining the five-day sequence of events that took place in California and in Washington, D.C. for President Reagan's state funeral
Comparison and Contrast *(Two objects, events, ideas, people, etcetera are compared and contrasted with one another.)*	Similarities of two subjects are described	Dissimilarities of the two subjects are identified	An essay comparing and contrasting the features of having dogs or having cats as house pets
Definition of a Term	A historical, scientific, literary or other term is presented	Attribution of specific features or characteristics, identification or analysis of parts, description of function, and/or examples	An encyclopedia entry defining and illustrating the chemical concept of pH
Persuasive Argument	The author expresses his or her opinion or point of view about a certain matter in a compelling and convincing manner		An argument for or against mandatory school uniforms
Narration	A narrative is a personal story. This may be an account or reminiscence, the recounting of an event or experience, or an anecdote.		An account of one's childhood summers spent at Camp Talkoda in the High Sierras

Sometimes a Critical Reading question asks you to identify the meaning of a short phrase that summarizes a method that the author is using to present his ideas. In this case, simply break down the phrase given and ask yourself if the passage matches the answer choice. Here are some examples:

- **Historical reflection:** "Historical" refers to significant events from the past. "Reflection" means thoughtful contemplation. This phrase refers to the author's contemplation of significant events from the past.

- **Personal reminiscence:** "Personal" signifies having to do with the self. "Reminiscence" is a remembrance, usually a nostalgic memory. A "personal reminiscence" would be the narrator's recollection of events that took place in his or her past.

- **Restatement of purpose:** To "restate" is to say again. The author's "purpose" is his theme or thesis. "Restatement of purpose" refers to the author's reiteration of his topic or primary point.

- **Data analysis:** "Data" refers to facts and statistics usually presented in a scientific manner. "Analysis" means to break down and examine. "Data analysis" would be the author's careful assessment of certain facts, figures and statistics.

- **Scientific conjecture:** "Scientific" means having to do with science. It also refers to precise, systematic and accurate methodology. "Conjecture" means speculation. "Scientific conjecture" is speculation based upon scientific results or principles. It constitutes an informed, "educated guess" about what might happen based upon the scientific facts presented.

- **Synthesis of prior claims:** "Synthesis" is combining, or synthesizing, diverse conceptions into a unified concept or statement. "Prior claims" are assertions or statements made previously. A "synthesis of prior claims" represents an author's attempt to combine different past assertions into one cohesive statement.

- **Testimony of experts:** "Testimony" is firsthand substantiation of certain facts. "Experts" are those who have gained respected proficiency in a certain field or area. "Testimony of experts" is the validation of certain facts by authorities in the field.

The author may also do the following:

- **Refute an argument:** To "refute" is to disagree with or dispute something. "Argument," in this case, would be that with which the author disagrees. To "refute an argument" is to systematically dispute a claim made by someone else.

- **Introduce a different perspective:** To "introduce" is to present new material. A "different perspective" is an alternative point of view about something. To "introduce a different perspective" is to present another point of view.

- **Question an assumption:** To "question" is to raise doubt about something. An "assumption" is a notion that people take for granted. When an author "questions an assumption," he is doubting its validity.

- **Challenge a premise:** To "challenge" is to dispute something. A "premise" is the basis of an argument. If the author challenges a premise, he is disputing the very core of an argument.

- **Cite authorities:** "To cite" means to quote. "Authorities" are people who have influence or expertise with respect to a given subject. "To cite authorities" would be to quote people who have important insights in a given area.

- **Highlight a debated controversy:** To "highlight" is to summarize. A "debated controversy" is an issue about which people have different opinions. To "highlight a debated controversy" would be to summarize the opposing viewpoints about a heated topic.

Question 9 from the sample passage *(see page 8; black stripe on outer edge of page)* refers to the author's organizational scheme or structural form:

- *Clean Up the Question by Crossing Out Unnecessary Words, Underlining Key Terms and Bracketing Passage Location:*

    9.   In [lines 33 – 45] (~~"Researchers also speculate…cannot function properly"~~), the author presents:

    (A)   a technical definition followed by functional analysis
    (B)   a general statement supported by a series of specific examples
    (C)   a scientific theory substantiated by data analysis
    (D)   a quotation followed by an interpretation
    (E)   an assertion countered by opposing arguments

- *Locate the Lines Needed and "Box the Text"*

The location for the text is referenced in the question, lines 33 – 45. The question states that we should start with the word "Researchers" and go to the end of line 45. (Because the question quotes specific material located within these lines, it is not necessary to include three lines before and after the lines cited.)

autoimmunity. <u>Researchers also speculate that certain mechanisms may trigger autoimmunity.</u> First, a substance
35   that is normally restricted to one part of the body, and therefore not usually exposed to the immune system, is released into other areas where it is attacked. Second, the immune system may mistake a component of the body for a similar foreign component. Third, cells of the body may
40   be altered in some way, either by drugs, infection, or some other environmental factor, so that they are no longer recognizable as "self" to the immune system. Fourth, the immune system itself may be damaged, such as by a genetic mutation, and therefore cannot function
45   properly.

- *Eliminate Bad Answer Choices*

The question asks which organizational technique the author uses in these lines. Start by simply reading the first sentence referred to: "Researchers also speculate that certain mechanisms may trigger autoimmunity." This is a general statement or assertion. The correct answer choice must refer to the author's initial use of a general statement or assertion, so we can eliminate choices (A), (C) and (D) from consideration.

Final Answer: Choices (B) and (E) start out the same: a "general statement" (choice (B)) is very similar to "an assertion" (choice (E)). The second sentence of the second paragraph reveals what will follow: "First, a substance that is normally restricted to one part of the body, and therefore not usually exposed to the immune system, is released into other areas where it is attacked." This is clearly an example of a possible trigger of autoimmunity, and it will probably be followed by other examples. By scanning the rest of the paragraph, you quickly spot the words "Second," "Third," and "Fourth" at the beginning of subsequent sentences that enumerate further examples of mechanisms that trigger autoimmunity. These are, therefore, a "series of specific examples," so the answer is (B).

✓ Critical Reading Strategy #16:
- ## The Approach for Dual Passages

One of the Critical Reading selections you can expect to encounter on the SAT will involve a "dual passage." This format involves two passages that offer different perspectives about the same subject. Longer dual passage sets are typically followed by 11 – 13 questions. To be successful on such dual passages, do the following:

1. **Read the beginning italicized lines that introduce the passages.** These lines may also contrast the perspectives of the two authors.
2. **Read the first passage,** underlining or circling important terms.
3. **Answer the questions about the first passage** (usually the first five or six questions).
4. **Read the second passage,** underlining or circling important terms.
5. **Answer the questions about the second passage** (usually the next five or six questions).
6. **Answer the last two or three questions.** Only these questions will require you to compare the two texts or to identify similarities or differences in the authors' presentation.

✓ Critical Reading Strategy #17:
- ## Know the Types of Reading Passages that You Will Encounter on the SAT

Passages for Critical Reading questions are excerpted from both fiction and non-fiction works. They are taken from a variety of literary formats, including the following:

- **Expository Non-Fiction:** Excerpts from books, biographies, academic journal articles, essays, literary criticism, catalogue introductions, reports, Supreme Court opinions, editorials, and speeches
- **Narrative Non-Fiction:** Selections from personal essays, memoirs, and autobiographies
- **Fiction:** Passages excerpted from novels or short stories

When SAT Critical Reading passages are selected, the test designers:

- seek to be politically correct, conforming to language and practices that do not offend the sensibilities of the diverse population of the world (particularly in matters of race or gender).
- select Critical Reading passages intended to broaden students' knowledge of and respect for other cultures, ethnic groups, and social conditions (multiculturalism).
- avoid controversial or derogatory passages or inflammatory points of view.

Passage Overview:

- There is usually at least one fiction passage on every SAT exam.
- Passages may be drawn from famous works of literature.
- Some passages are very short, consisting of two to four sentences (100 words) followed by one or two questions.

CRITICAL READING

CHAPTER 3 SUMMARY

1. **Paraphrasing questions** ask you to synthesize and summarize portions of the text. The synopsis stated in the correct answer choice must be an accurate re-statement that addresses key points.

2. **Inference questions** require you to draw a conclusion based on what is stated in the passage. What you can infer is suggested, but not directly stated, in the passage. The conclusion you draw must be based entirely upon what is stated in the passage. This means your answer must be a reasonable deduction.

3. **Vocabulary-in-Context questions** ask for the meaning of a word as used in a given portion of the text. The correct synonym is usually a secondary meaning of the word, so synonyms for the word's primary meaning can usually be ruled out.

4. **The SAT's Critical Reading questions require students to be familiar with literary techniques and rhetorical devices** commonly encountered in a high school literature course.

5. **Critical Reading questions for non-fiction passages may ask you to identify the author's organizational scheme, technique or structural form.**

6. **Dual passages present different perspectives regarding a common topic.** For long dual passage sets (a pair of passages followed by ten or more questions), treat each passage separately, reading one passage at a time and then answering the questions about it. For such selections only the last two or three questions will refer to both passages.

7. **Passages for Critical Reading questions are excerpted from both fiction and non-fiction works.** The SAT usually includes a fiction passage that could be taken from a famous work of literature. Short passages (approximately 100 words in length) are followed by one or two questions.

Critical Reading
Chapter 4

Practice Passages with Accompanying Questions:

- Five short passages

- Non-fiction passage

- Fiction passage

- Dual passage set

Vocabulary-in-Context Practice Exercises

PRACTICE EXERCISES:
SHORT PASSAGES & QUESTIONS
(NEW ON THE SAT)

The Galileo spacecraft was named after the first
astronomer who turned a telescope skyward and
transformed Jupiter from a myth-inspiring, bright point of
light into a giant, turbulent world that appeared as a solar
(5) system unto itself. In the early 1600s, Galileo Galilei not
only identified Jupiter as a planet, but also saw four
moons orbiting it. This view is now accessible to anyone
with a decent pair of binoculars, but the discovery was
certainly something of significance at a time when many
(10) believed that everything in the universe orbited the Earth.
As of this writing, a dizzying total of 61 moons have been
discovered around Jupiter – a number which has doubled
in just the past two years and still has room to grow.

1. The primary purpose of this passage is to:

(A) discuss the role of the Galileo spacecraft in
discovering more about Jupiter and its moons

(B) emphasize the importance of Galileo's contributions to astronomy

(C) demonstrate that the arrangement of Jupiter and
its moons is analogous to our solar system

(D) convey our current knowledge of Jupiter and its
moons as compared with Galileo's first discoveries about this planetary system

(E) suggest that it is impossible to ascertain the
number of moons that truly orbit Jupiter

2. The author states that "this view is now accessible to anyone with a decent pair of binoculars"
(lines 7 – 8) in order to:

(A) discount the discoveries that Galileo first made
about Jupiter

(B) imply that the lenses in powerful binoculars are
better than those found in many telescopes

(C) acknowledge that significant advances have been
made in optic technology since Galileo's time

(D) promote amateur astronomy

(E) introduce the idea that planetariums that are open
to the public may become obsolete

The conspicuous absence of the pronounced
militaristic tendencies in Minoan society which are such a
prominent feature of Mycenaean culture raises the
obvious question of how an emerging Minoan élite
(5) established or maintained its authority. It may well be that
the manipulation of religious ideology may have lain at
the very heart of the Minoan rulership's power, in which
case correlations between changes in cult practice and the
emergence of the state are to be anticipated. Relatively
(10) little is presently known about Minoan religious practices
during the Early Minoan and Middle Minoan periods so
that in this area, as in studies of settlement patterns and
ceramic chronology, much work needs to be done.

3. The main idea of this passage is best stated by
which of the following?

(A) prehistoric archaeological findings regarding
Minoan and Mycenaean civilizations

(B) the contrast between Minoan and Mycenaean
sources of authority

(C) the lack of a military presence in Minoan society

(D) unfinished archaeological studies of the Early
Minoan and Middle Minoan periods

(E) uncertainty regarding the methodology by which
Minoan leadership established or sustained its
power

4. Minoan rulers may have reshaped religious ideology in order to:

(A) introduce the importance of civic responsibility

(B) underscore the importance of reverence for deity

(C) insure the citizenry's compliance with authority

(D) suggest that the Minoan state should be protected
by military force

(E) stop controversial cult practices

As concerns in recent years have grown about global warming caused by carbon-dioxide emissions, scientists have begun to reconsider electricity as a fuel for vehicles. But today's drivers expect a vehicle that is fuel *(5)* efficient, and a fuel that is readily available in numerous locations and allows "instant" refueling. Though electric cars are fairly efficient, they require frequent refueling, and the process is far from instantaneous. They're expensive, too, since normal use causes their $2,000 lead-*(10)* acid batteries to wear out in just a few years. And, ironically, electric cars do very little to reduce carbon dioxide emissions because most electricity in the U.S. is generated by burning coal and other fossil fuels. To gain consumer acceptance, the car of the future will need to *(15)* balance the benefits of electric cars with consumer demands for distance and dynamo. The hybrid electric vehicle holds promise as a solution to both these needs.

5. It can be inferred that which of the following would help reduce global warming?

(A) restrict the manufacture of electric vehicles to compact sized cars

(B) obtain the electricity needed to operate electric cars from renewable energy sources such as hydroelectric power

(C) replace the lead-acid batteries with alternative fuel cells

(D) build electric cars that require less frequent refueling

(E) turn the car into a hybrid electric vehicle that would include the addition of a small internal combustion engine

6. According to the passage, which of the following best states what consumers expect with respect to electric cars?

(A) inexpensive batteries, power and comfort

(B) instant refueling, low maintenance and long battery life

(C) fuel capacity, ease of operation, and luxury

(D) readily available fuel, cost effectiveness, and reduced carbon dioxide emissions

(E) fuel efficiency, convenience, and strong performance

The responsibility of a juror can best be summed up in a statement by John Jay, the first Chief Justice of the U.S. Supreme Court. He stated, in 1789, that "The jury has a right to judge both the law as well as the fact in *(5)* controversy." This means that a juror judges both the merits of the case and the law upon which the case is based. A juror, by voting not guilty, can literally void a law. The misconception is that any law passed by a legislature constitutes the law of the land. Theoretically, a *(10)* single juror can nullify a law concerning gun control, drug regulation, hate speech, or other legislation.

7. The passage implies that jury nullification results in which of the following:

(A) a weaker legislature

(B) a greater number of jury verdicts are overturned on appeal

(C) laws are irregularly enforced, as different juries may choose to apply or not apply them in their decisions

(D) an increased number of citizens avoids jury duty

(E) more mistrials occur due to hung juries

8. As used in line 10, the word "nullify" most nearly means:

(A) misinterpret

(B) undermine

(C) spurn

(D) invalidate

(E) overturn

The artistic movement of Surrealism took place between 1924 and 1940 in France. Often categorized as an elite clique, it reflected artistic sensitivity to recent political changes occurring in the Western world. The
(5) death and destruction during the First World War, for instance, had shattered the confidence of many in the West's ability to progress benevolently. Additionally, revolutionary discoveries, such as Sigmund Freud's identification of the unconscious mind, and Albert
(10) Einstein's theories regarding time and space had left the masses feeling uncertain about humanity and the world around them. In reaction to this, Surrealist artists created a medium of images that articulated such disturbing social changes which words alone failed to express.

9. The author most likely includes references to Sigmund Freud and Albert Einstein in order to:

(A) provide a time frame reference for the introduction of Surrealism

(B) contrast the death and destruction of the First World War with important scientific achievements

(C) explain that modern science was at odds with Surrealism

(D) provide examples of radical theories and discoveries to which Surrealists responded

(E) emphasize the intellectual atmosphere in which Surrealism was born

10. As used in line 13, the word "medium" most nearly means:

(A) middle
(B) mode
(C) intermediate
(D) canvas
(E) assortment

PRACTICE EXERCISES:
LONGER PASSAGES & QUESTIONS

Questions 1 – 6 are based on the following passage.

The following is William Faulkner's 1950 acceptance speech upon receiving the Nobel Prize for Literature.

I feel that this award was not made to me as a man, but to my work – a life's work in the agony and sweat of the human spirit, not for glory and least of all for profit, but to create out of the materials of the human
(5) spirit something which did not exist before. So this award is only mine in trust. It will not be difficult to find a dedication for the money part of it commensurate with the purpose and significance of its origin. But I would like to do the same with the acclaim too, by using this moment as
(10) a pinnacle from which I might be listened to by the young men and women already dedicated to the same anguish and travail, among whom is already that one who will some day stand here where I am standing.

Our tragedy today is a general and universal
(15) physical fear so long sustained by now that we can even bear it. There are no longer problems of the spirit. There is only the question: When will I be blown up? Because of this, the young man or woman writing today has forgotten the problems of the human heart in conflict with
(20) itself which alone can make good writing because only that is worth writing about, worth the agony and the sweat.

He must learn them again. He must teach himself that the basest of all things is to be afraid; and, teaching
(25) himself that, forget it forever, leaving no room in his workshop for anything but the old verities and truths of the heart, the old universal truths lacking which any story is ephemeral and doomed – love and honor and pity and pride and compassion and sacrifice. Until he does so, he
(30) labors under a curse. He writes not of love but of lust, of defeats in which nobody loses anything of value, of victories without hope and, worst of all, without pity or compassion. His griefs grieve on no universal bones, leaving no scars. He writes not of the heart but of the
(35) glands.

Until he relearns these things, he will write as though he stood among and watched the end of man. I decline to accept the end of man. It is easy enough to say that man is immortal simply because he will endure: that
(40) when the last dingdong of doom has clanged and faded from the last worthless rock hanging tideless in the last red and dying evening, that even then there will still be one more sound: that of his puny inexhaustible voice, still talking. I refuse to accept this. I believe that man will not
(45) merely endure: he will prevail. He is immortal, not

because he alone among creatures has an inexhaustible voice, but because he has a soul, a spirit capable of compassion and sacrifice and endurance. The poet's, the writer's, duty is to write about these things. It is his
(50) privilege to help man endure by lifting his heart, by reminding him of the courage and honor and hope and pride and compassion and pity and sacrifice which have been the glory of his past. The poet's voice need not merely be the record of man, it can be one of the props,
(55) the pillars to help him endure and prevail.

1. In the first paragraph of his speech, Faulkner indicates that his remarks are aimed to which of the following groups:

(A) those who have lost touch with important values such as love, honor, pity, pride, compassion and sacrifice
(B) young writers
(C) Nobel Prize committee members
(D) atomic scientists who have brought the world to the brink of nuclear destruction
(E) citizens who are afraid of current world conditions

2. According to Faulkner, what alone is "worth writing about" (line 21)?

(A) man's presumed immortality
(B) universal physical fear
(C) the glory of man's past
(D) the present human condition
(E) the human heart in conflict with itself

3. It can be reasonably inferred that Faulkner's remarks are made in the context of which of the following historical events?

(A) North Korea's invasion of South Korea in 1950
(B) the Cuban Missile Crisis in 1961
(C) Hitler's invasion of Europe from 1936 – 1942
(D) the atomic bombings of Japan in 1945 that ended World War II
(E) the Cold War during the 1950s between the United States and the Soviet Union

4. In stating, "He writes not of the heart but of the glands," (lines 34 – 35) Faulkner means:

(A) modern writers are more interested in the body's circulatory system than in the endocrine system

(B) Faulkner does not approve of the plots and characters occupying present-day fiction

(C) contemporary writers have forsaken passion in their work, adopting a mechanical, empty approach

(D) young writers remain impacted by hormonal factors

(E) universal truths have eluded current writers

5. Faulkner believes that "man will not merely endure: he will prevail" because:

(A) man alone among creatures has an inexhaustible voice

(B) man has avoided extinction that could have been caused by nuclear destruction

(C) man has a soul that possesses essential spiritual capabilities

(D) man always prevails against nature

(E) man understands important universal truths

6. The word "props" in line 54 most nearly means:

(A) stage objects

(B) costumes

(C) columns

(D) factors

(E) supports

Questions 1 – 7 are based on the following passage.

In the following excerpt from a novel, the narrator lives with his grandparents in Nebraska next door to the Shimerda family, who emigrated from Bohemia and now operate a farm.

Mrs. Shimerda asked me to stay for supper. After Ambrosch and Antonia had washed the field dust from their hands and faces at the wash-basin by the kitchen door, we sat down at the oilcloth-covered table. Mrs.
(5)   Shimerda ladled meal mush out of an iron pot and poured milk on it. After the mush we had fresh bread and sorghum molasses, and coffee with the cake that had been kept warm in the feathers. Antonia and Ambrosch were talking in Bohemian; disputing about which of them had
(10)   done more ploughing that day. Mrs. Shimerda egged them on, chuckling while she gobbled her food.

Presently Ambrosch said sullenly in English: "You take them ox tomorrow and try the sod plough. Then you not be so smart."

(15)   His sister laughed. "Don't be mad. I know it's awful hard work for break sod. I milk the cow for you tomorrow, if you want."

Mrs. Shimerda turned quickly to me. "That cow not give so much milk like what your grandpa say. If he
(20)   make talk about fifteen dollars, I send him back the cow."

"He doesn't talk about the fifteen dollars," I exclaimed indignantly. "He doesn't find fault with people."

"He say I break his saw when we build, and I
(25)   never," grumbled Ambrosch.

I knew he had broken the saw, and then hid it and lied about it. I began to wish I had not stayed for supper. Everything was disagreeable to me. Antonia ate so noisily now, like a man, and she yawned often at the
(30)   table and kept stretching her arms over her head, as if they ached. Grandmother had said, "Heavy field work'll spoil that girl. She'll lose all her nice ways and get rough ones." She had lost them already.

After supper I rode home through the sad, soft
(35)   spring twilight. Since winter I had seen very little of Antonia. She was out in the fields from sunup until sundown. If I rode over to see her where she was ploughing, she stopped at the end of a row to chat for a moment, then gripped her plough-handles, clucked to her
(40)   team, and waded on down the furrow, making me feel that she was now grown up and had no time for me. On Sundays she helped her mother make garden or sewed all day. Grandfather was pleased with Antonia. When we complained of her, he only smiled and said, "She will
(45)   help some fellow get ahead in the world."

Nowadays Tony could talk of nothing but the prices of things, or how much she could lift and endure. She was too proud of her strength. I knew, too, that Ambrosch put upon her some chores a girl ought not to
(50)   do, and that the farm-hands around the country joked in a nasty way about it. Whenever I saw her come up the furrow, shouting to her beasts, sunburned, sweaty, her dress open at the neck, and her throat and chest dust plastered, I used to think of the tone in which poor Mr.
(55)   Shimerda, who could say so little, yet managed to say so much when he exclaimed, "My Antonia!"

1.   In the first paragraph, the supper described includes which of the following items?

(A)   bread, cake, eggs, molasses, and mush
(B)   chicken, eggs, molasses, and mush
(C)   bread, cake, molasses, and turkey
(D)   bread, chicken, mush, and turkey
(E)   bread, cake, molasses, and mush

2.   The character Ambrosch is:

(A)   a paid field hand
(B)   Mrs. Shimerda's nephew
(C)   Antonia's brother
(D)   the narrator's brother
(E)   the Shimerdas' neighbor

3.   The narrator regrets staying for supper (lines 27 – 28) because:

(A)   Ambrosch has just lied and Antonia is behaving in a masculine manner
(B)   the narrator is upset about the broken saw
(C)   the narrator is afraid of Mrs. Shimerda
(D)   the Shimerdas are not well mannered
(E)   the Shimerdas are engaged in a noisy dispute

4. It can be inferred that Ambrosch's motivation for lying about the saw (lines 24 – 25) is to:

(A) escape punishment from Mrs. Shimerda

(B) reinforce Mrs. Shimerda's accusation against the narrator's grandfather

(C) defend the narrator's grandfather against Mrs. Shimerda

(D) avoid replacing the broken saw

(E) prove to the narrator that cows are more valuable than saws

5. The narrator's reference to Antonia as "Tony" (line 46):

(A) stems from the Shimerdas' casual style

(B) is ironic, as the nickname "Tony" is usually used as a male nickname, and the narrator abhors Antonia's loss of femininity

(C) would clearly annoy Mrs. Shimerda if spoken aloud

(D) illustrates the common use of nicknames in the Midwest

(E) is the narrator's attempt to "Americanize" Antonia's name

6. When the narrator sensed that Antonia "was now grown up and had no time for me" (lines 40 – 41), his interpretation was based upon Antonia's:

(A) recent physical growth

(B) willingness to remain on the family farm

(C) diligent and independent dedication to performing her chores

(D) unwavering assistance to her family during difficult times

(E) acquisition of respect from her elders

7. Mr. Shimerda's attitude toward Antonia is that of:

(A) Admiration subdued by regret

(B) Unrequited shame

(C) Indifference tinged with sadness

(D) Unequivocal pride

(E) Bitter acceptance

Questions 1 – 13 are based on the following passages.

Below are excerpts of the opinions of two Supreme Court justices concerning the 1972 United States Supreme Court case Furman v. Georgia, in which the Court held that the imposition and carrying out of the death penalty constituted cruel and unusual punishment in violation of the Eighth and Fourteenth Amendments of the United States Constitution. Passage 1 is excerpted from Justice Byron White's opinion concurring with the court majority. Passage 2 is excerpted from Justice Harry Blackmun's dissenting opinion.

Passage 1

I begin with what I consider a near truism: that the death penalty could so seldom be imposed that it would cease to be a credible deterrent or measurably to contribute to any other end of
(5)   punishment in the criminal justice system. It is perhaps true that no matter how infrequently those convicted of rape or murder are executed, the penalty so imposed is not disproportionate to the crime and those executed may deserve exactly what they
(10) received. It would also be clear that executed defendants are finally and completely incapacitated from again committing rape or murder or any other crime. But when imposition of the penalty reaches a certain degree of infrequency, it would be very
(15) doubtful that any existing general need for retribution would be measurably satisfied. Nor could it be said with confidence that society's need for specific deterrence justifies death for so few when for so many in like circumstances life imprisonment or shorter
(20) prison terms are judged sufficient, or that community values are measurably reinforced by authorizing a penalty so rarely invoked.

Most important, a major goal of the criminal law – to deter others by punishing the convicted
(25) criminal – would not be substantially served where the penalty is so seldom invoked that it ceases to be the credible threat essential to influence the conduct of others. For present purposes I accept the morality and utility of punishing one person to influence another. I
(30) accept also the effectiveness of punishment generally and need not reject the death penalty as a more effective deterrent than a lesser punishment. But common sense and experience tell us that seldom enforced laws become ineffective measures for
(35) controlling human conduct and that the death penalty, unless imposed with sufficient frequency, will make little contribution to deterring those crimes for which it may be exacted.

It is also my judgment that this point has
(40) been reached with respect to capital punishment as it is presently administered under the statutes involved in these cases. Concededly, it is difficult to prove as a general proposition that capital punishment, however administered, more effectively serves the ends of the
(45) criminal law than does imprisonment. But however that may be, I cannot avoid the conclusion that as the statutes before us are now administered, the penalty is so infrequently imposed that the threat of execution is too attenuated to be of substantial service to criminal
(50) justice.

Passage 2

Cases such as these provide for me an excruciating agony of the spirit. I yield to no one in the depth of my distaste, antipathy, and, indeed, abhorrence, for the death penalty, with all its aspects
(55) of physical distress and fear and of moral judgment exercised by finite minds. That distaste is buttressed by a belief that capital punishment serves no useful purpose that can be demonstrated. For me, it violates childhood's training and life's experiences, and is not
(60) compatible with the philosophical convictions I have been able to develop. It is antagonistic to any sense of "reverence for life." Were I a legislator, I would vote against the death penalty for the policy reasons argued by counsel for the respective petitioners and expressed
(65) and adopted in the several opinions filed by the Justices who vote to reverse these judgments.

As I have said above, were I a legislator, I would do all I could to sponsor and to vote for legislation abolishing the death penalty. And were I
(70) the chief executive of a sovereign State, I would be sorely tempted to exercise executive clemency as Governor Rockefeller of Arkansas did recently just before he departed from office. There – on the Legislative Branch of the State or Federal
(75) Government, and secondarily, on the Executive Branch – is where the authority and responsibility for this kind of action lies. The authority should not be taken over by the judiciary in the modern guise of an Eighth Amendment issue.

(80) I do not sit on these cases, however, as a legislator, responsive, at least in part, to the will of constituents. Our task here, as must so frequently be emphasized and re-emphasized, is to pass upon the constitutionality of legislation that has been enacted
(85) and that is challenged. This is the sole task for judges. We should not allow our personal preferences as to the wisdom of legislative and congressional action, or our distaste for such action, to guide our judicial

decision in cases such as these. The temptations to
(90) cross that policy line are very great. In fact, as today's
decision reveals, they are almost irresistible.

Although personally I may rejoice at the
Court's result, I find it difficult to accept or to justify
as a matter of history, of law, or of constitutional
(95) pronouncement. I fear the Court has overstepped. It
has sought and has achieved an end.

1. The word "measurably" in line 16 most nearly
   means:

   (A) numerically
   (B) evidently
   (C) obviously
   (D) significantly
   (E) inconsequentially

2. As stated in Passage 1, which of the following
   best states Justice White's chief objection to the
   imposition and carrying out of the death penalty?

   (A) it is cruel and unusual punishment and is there-
       fore in violation of the Eighth Amendment of the
       United States Constitution
   (B) the sentence is disproportionate to the crime of rape
   (C) it does not allow for the possibility that some death
       row inmates may be candidates for rehabilitation
   (D) it has not been proven whether or not the death
       penalty is a more significant deterrent to crime
       than life imprisonment
   (E) it is invoked so rarely that it ceases to be a true
       threat in deterring crime

3. The phrase "morality and utility" in lines 28 – 29
   refers to:

   (A) ethics and application
   (B) values and significance
   (C) ideology and value
   (D) ethics and effectiveness
   (E) principles and advantage

4. In Passage 1, Justice White questions the role of
   capital punishment in the context of which of the
   following?

   (A) the method by which it is imposed
   (B) its application in the criminal justice system
   (C) the rights of victims of violent crimes
   (D) the rights of the accused
   (E) its concurrence with the Constitution

5. As used in line 49, the word "attenuated" most
   nearly means:

   (A) violent
   (B) controversial
   (C) diminished
   (D) inconsistent
   (E) disturbing

6. According to Passage 1, Justice White believes
   that all of the following are true about the death
   penalty EXCEPT:

   (A) violent criminals will be unable to commit future
       crimes
   (B) the death penalty is not too extreme for the crime
       committed
   (C) it is a more effective deterrent than other punish-
       ments
   (D) community values are not significantly supported
       by the availability of the death penalty
   (E) it is uncertain whether the death penalty fulfills
       any perceived need for retribution

7. The "excruciating agony of the spirit" (line 52) that Justice Blackmun experiences in hearing capital punishment cases arises from:

(A) the conflict presented by Justice Blackmun's tremendous personal aversion to capital punishment coupled with his belief that the judiciary has no true authority to rule on this issue

(B) the overload of death penalty cases that the Supreme Court has been presented

(C) Justice Blackmun's belief that the death penalty constitutes cruel and unusual punishment

(D) the hostile debate that invariably ensues among the Supreme Court Justices in Eighth Amendment cases

(E) Justice Blackmun's conviction that a society that kills is hypocritical about murder

8. The word "buttressed" in line 56 most nearly means:

(A) confirmed

(B) maintained

(C) undermined

(D) reinforced

(E) preserved

9. In paragraph one of Passage 2, Justice Blackmun concedes that he believes all but which of the following about the death penalty?

(A) limited human intellect assesses moral judgment in its imposition

(B) no useful purpose is effectively served by imposing the death penalty

(C) the death penalty shows no regard for life itself

(D) the concept of the death penalty runs counter to his childhood training, life experiences and philosophical convictions

(E) it qualifies constitutionally as cruel and unusual punishment

10. The phrase "executive clemency" as used in line 71 refers to:

(A) a federal official's right to grant a stay of execution

(B) Congress's power to overturn a sentence of capital punishment

(C) a state governor's authority to halt an execution

(D) a death row inmate's right to exhaust all remedies in the appeals process

(E) a state clemency board's hearing prior to the execution of any death row inmate

11. According to Justice Blackmun, the "sole task for judges" (line 85) of the Supreme Court is to:

(A) engage in judicial activism in shaping social policy

(B) judge the constitutionality of laws enacted by Congress

(C) encourage the executive branch to veto questionable legislation

(D) reshape legislation to fit the Constitution

(E) make certain that cases heard before the Supreme Court are primarily concerned with upholding the Bill of Rights

12. In his opinion as stated in Passage 2, Justice Blackmun implies which of the following?

(A) the Supreme Court should exercise less power than it does in certain cases

(B) the judiciary should not decide whether certain crimes qualify for capital punishment

(C) it is the domain of the legislative or executive branches of the government to determine whether or not capital punishment is lawful

(D) the Supreme Court does not have the authority to hear cases that concern the Eighth Amendment

(E) if he were a legislator, Justice Blackmun would vote to overturn the death penalty

13. In comparing Passage 1 with Passage 2, which of the following is true?

(A) Justice White (Passage 1) has a greater personal dislike for the death penalty than does Justice Blackmun (Passage 2)

(B) both justices believe that the death penalty serves a useful purpose in the criminal justice system

(C) neither justice believes that murderers or rapists facing execution deserve this punishment

(D) evaluation of the death penalty with respect to the Fourteenth Amendment is more significant in Justice Blackmun's opinion (Passage 2) than in Justice White's (Passage 1)

(E) neither Justice Blackmun nor Justice White bases his opinion solely upon his interpretation of the Eighth Amendment of the Constitution

**PRACTICE EXERCISES:
VOCABULARY-IN-CONTEXT**

1. The defense attorney will sandwich an appointment with the accused criminal between his 1:30 p.m. and 3:00 p.m. jail visits with convicted felons.

    In the sentence above, the word "sandwich" means:

    (A) bread
    (B) pack
    (C) make
    (D) squeeze in
    (E) cancel

2. He embroidered his explanation with details that were obviously fabricated.

    In the sentence above, the word "embroidered" means:

    (A) sewed
    (B) mended
    (C) embellished
    (D) complicated
    (E) narrated

3. The reckless abandon with which he drove made him unpopular on the NASCAR circuit.

    In the sentence above, the word "abandon" means:

    (A) desertion
    (B) alone
    (C) speed
    (D) lack of restraint
    (E) caution

4. The trade winds are stronger than one would expect, and they can even buffet large cruise ships.

    In the sentence above, the word "buffet" means:

    (A) cafeteria
    (B) dine
    (C) nourish
    (D) sail
    (E) thrash

5. The carburetor is an important constituent of an automobile's engine.

    In the sentence above, the word "constituent" means:

    (A) voter
    (B) citizen
    (C) purifier
    (D) gauge
    (E) component

6. The narrow intersection of the two related wolf populations showed how few characteristics they had in common.

    In the sentence above, the word "intersection" means:

    (A) street corner
    (B) traffic
    (C) cross-section
    (D) union
    (E) group

7. The professor's patent favoritism of the boys in the class caused several girls to drop the course.

    In the sentence above, the word "patent" means:

    (A) trademark
    (B) copyright
    (C) obvious
    (D) unwanted
    (E) unethical

8. A rash of burglaries occurred in Chicago immediately after the riots.

    In the sentence above, the word "rash" means:

    (A) allergy
    (B) reaction
    (C) hasty
    (D) series
    (E) frenzy

9. The examination his gastroenterologist ordered indicated the presence of occult blood.

    In the sentence above, the word "occult" means:

(A) sinister

(B) psychic

(C) dark

(D) hidden

(E) excess

10. The businessman's motives were so transparent that almost anyone could anticipate the nature of his next venture.

    In the sentence above, the word "transparent" means:

(A) invisible

(B) opaque

(C) translucent

(D) apparent

(E) confused

SHORT PASSAGES: ANSWER EXPLANATIONS

Question #1: (D)

➤ *Question Type:* Main Idea

The passage does not address the role of the Galileo spacecraft or the impossibility of discovering the true number of Jupiter's moons, so choices (A) and (E) can be eliminated. Choice (C) is stated in the passage but is a detail, not the primary purpose. Galileo's contributions are one facet of the passage (choice (B)), but the text also outlines our current knowledge of Jupiter. The answer is (D).

Question #2: (C)

➤ *Question Type:* Specific Detail

Galileo's discoveries about Jupiter are viewed with admiration; eliminate choice (A). There is no comparison of the lenses in binoculars with those in telescopes; eliminate choice (B). Neither amateur astronomy nor planetariums are mentioned in the passage; eliminate choices (D) and (E). The author makes this statement to contrast the state of astronomy during Galileo's time with its present state. The answer is (C).

Question #3: (E)

➤ *Question Type:* Main Idea

Choices (A) and (B) can be eliminated because both refer to the Mycenaeans, a culture briefly mentioned in line 3 but unrelated to the main idea. Choices (C) and (D) both refer to specific details, not the main idea. The passage addresses a curiosity about how the Minoan leadership established control without a military presence. The best answer is (E).

Question #4: (C)

➤ *Question Type:* Specific Detail

"Reverence for deity" (choice (B)), "the Minoan state should be protected by military force" (choice (D)), and "controversial cult practices" (choice (E)) are not mentioned or implied by the passage. While Minoan rulers probably supported a show of civic responsibility (choice (A)), their goal with respect to manipulating religious beliefs would have been to assure the people's submission to their authority. The answer is (C).

Question #5: (B)

➤ *Question Type:* Inference

Choice (A) can be eliminated because there is no suggestion that the size of the vehicle might influence global warming. Lead-acid batteries are expensive (lines 8 – 10), but the text does not suggest that replacing them with alternative fuel cells would help reduce global warming; eliminate choice (C). Choice (D) can be eliminated because less frequent refueling (lines 4 – 8) represents a consumer convenience but not an environmental gain. Although the passage indicates that the "hybrid electric vehicle holds promise" (lines 16 – 17), the promise is for the consumer and not the environment. The addition of an internal combustion engine burning gasoline would add to carbon dioxide emissions and hence to global warming; choice (E) is incorrect. The passage indicates that global warming is caused by carbon dioxide emissions (line 2), and further that the current problem with electricity is that it "is generated by burning coal or other fossil fuels" (lines 12 – 13). It can be inferred that if the electricity were obtained from alternative sources, global warming may be reduced. The answer is (B).

Question #6: (E)

➤ *Question Type:* Specific Detail

"Comfort" (choice (A)), "low maintenance" (choice (B)), and "luxury" (choice (C)) are not mentioned in the passage; all three should be eliminated. Reduction of carbon dioxide emissions (choice (D)) is environmentally desirable, but it is not necessarily a top consumer concern. Choice (E) best summarizes consumers' expectations with respect to electric vehicles: "drivers expect a car that is fuel efficient and a fuel that is readily available in numerous locations" (lines 4 – 6) and consumers demand "distance and dynamo" (lines 15 – 16).

Question #7: (C)

➤ *Question Type:* Inference

According to the passage, "a juror judges both the merits of a case and the law upon which the case is based" (lines 5 – 7). The result of this is that "theoretically, a single juror can nullify a law" (lines 9 – 10). This does not imply a weaker legislature (choice (A)), an increase in overturned jury verdicts (choice (B)), more citizens avoiding jury duty (choice (D)), or more mistrials (choice (E)). Because different jurors may appraise laws differently, certain laws may or may not be enforced in various cases. (C) is the correct inference.

Question #8: (D)

➤ *Question Type:* Vocabulary-in-Context
The sentence in which the word "nullify" appears does not make sense if choices (B), (C) and (E) are used as substitutions; these answers can be eliminated. This is a somewhat challenging vocabulary-in-context question. It is necessary to refer to previous context clues in the passage to understand what, exactly, "nullify" means. Lines 7 – 8 state: "A juror, by voting not guilty, can literally void a law." This leads one to conclude that the words "void" and "nullify" are synonyms. Jury nullification means that jury decisions can nullify, or void the law in certain cases. The best additional synonym for these words is "invalidate" (choice (D)), not "misinterpret" (choice (A)).

Question #9: (D)

➤ *Question Type:* Specific Detail
Lines 8 – 10 show that the references to Freud and Einstein provide examples: "revolutionary discoveries, such as Sigmund Freud's identification of the unconscious mind, and Albert Einstein's theory regarding time and space…." Lines 12 – 14 explain the Surrealists' response to such revolutionary theories: "In reaction to this, Surrealist artists created a medium of images…." Reference is made to Freud and Einstein as examples of scientists whose revolutionary discoveries were responded to by Surrealists. The answer is (D).

Question #10: (E)

➤ *Question Type:* Vocabulary-in-Context
Choices (A), (B) and (C) all contain words that are synonymous with the primary meaning of the word "medium" that are incorrect in this context. The word "canvas" (choice (D)) is a word associated with art, but it not an appropriate substitute for "medium." The best synonym for "medium" in this context is "assortment," choice (E).

ANSWER EXPLANATIONS: WILLIAM FAULKNER'S NOBEL LECTURE

Question #1: (B)

➤ *Question Type:* Specific Detail
The first paragraph does not directly refer to or imply an audience represented by answer choices (A), (D) or (E). While the opening lines of Faulkner's speech may very well be directed to Nobel Prize committee members (choice (B)), lines 9 – 12 indicate that the balance of Faulkner's speech is directed to young writers. The answer is (B).

Question #2: (E)

➤ *Question Type:* Specific Detail
A quick reading of lines 17 – 22 reveals that none of the answer choices (A) – (D) are mentioned. These lines refer to "the human heart in conflict with itself which alone can make good writing." The answer is (E).

Question #3: (D)

➤ *Question Type:* Inference
The italicized introduction refers to 1950 as the year that Faulkner gave this speech. Choices (B) and (E) refer to events that occurred thereafter, so these choices are incorrect. Line 17 indicates that people were preoccupied with the possibility of being "blown up." Although choices (A) and (C) both refer to warfare, choice (D) refers specifically to the then recent explosion of nuclear bombs. (D) is the best answer.

Question #4: (C)

➤ *Question Type:* Interpretation of Figurative Language
Choices (A) and (D) can be eliminated immediately, as they refer to the literal rather than figurative interpretation of the statement. Choice (B) can also be eliminated, as Faulkner makes no reference to the plots and characters of present-day fiction. The problem Faulkner outlines is not that current writers do not understand universal truths (choice (E)). Faulkner is concerned that fear has caused writers to abandon the heartrending, passionate process required to write great literature. (C) is the best answer.

Question #5: (C)

> *Question Type:* Specific Detail

Faulkner is not talking about man's physical survival with respect to nuclear destruction or nature, so choices (B) and (D) are incorrect. Faulkner's discussion of "universal truths" (choice (E)) in line 27 relates to the content of good literature, not to man's ultimate triumph. Lines 45 – 47 state that man is "immortal… not because he…has an inexhaustible voice," so choice (A) can also be eliminated. The text indicates that man will prevail because he is immortal. He is immortal "because he has a soul, a spirit capable of compassion and sacrifice and endurance" (lines 47 – 48). This is best stated by choice (C).

Question #6: (E)

> *Question Type:* Vocabulary-in-Context

The word "props" is not being used to refer to items used in theatre, so choices (A) and (B) can be eliminated. Choice (D) does not make sense in the sentence. Choice (C) appears to be an alternative meaning of "pillars," a word that appears in this same sentence. In lines 54 – 55, the phrase "it can be one of the props, the pillars" indicates that here props are the same thing as pillars – something that supports or buttresses. Choice (E) is best.

ANSWER EXPLANATIONS: PASSAGE FROM NOVEL (MY ANTONIA)

Question #1: (E)

> *Question Type:* Specific Detail

In the first paragraph, the characters are eating mush, bread, molasses, and cake. Words such as "feathers," "egged," and "gobbled" may have distracted you from choosing the correct answer.

Question #2: (C)

> *Question Type:* Specific Detail

"His sister laughed" (line 15) refers to Antonia's laughing at Ambrosch during their dispute about the farm work; therefore, Ambrosch is Antonia's brother. Ambrosch and Antonia's mother is Mrs. Shimerda, and their father is Mr. Shimerda.

Question #3: (A)

> *Question Type:* Inference

The narrator is referring to the immediately preceding incident in which Ambrosch lies about the saw and the ensuing description of Antonia's noisy eating, her yawning, and her stretching. After Antonia's grandmother states her concern that her granddaughter might "'lose all her nice ways and get rough ones'" (line 31), the narrator unhappily concludes (line 32) that Antonia "had lost them already."

Question #4: (B)

> *Question Type:* Inference

Ambrosch is countering the narrator's argument that the narrator's grandfather "doesn't find fault with people." By doing this, Ambrosch is also reinforcing Mrs. Shimerda's claim that the grandfather sold a bad cow to the Shimerdas.

Question #5: (B)

> *Question Type:* Synthesis

Throughout the passage, the narrator is dismayed and annoyed by what he perceives as Antonia's growing masculinity. It is ironic that he would call her by a male nickname version of her name.

Question #6: (C)

> *Question Type:* Specific Detail

In lines 35 – 41, the narrator laments seeing less of Antonia because she is working on the farm all of the time. When he comes to visit, she is too busy to stop long enough to have a satisfying conversation with the narrator and simply carries on with her responsibilities. In conclusion, he states, "She was now grown up and had no time for me."

Question #7: (D)

> *Question Type:* Inference

Lines 43 – 45 indicate that Mr. Shimerda has a positive view of Antonia: "Grandfather was pleased with Antonia. When we complained of her, he only smiled and said, 'She will help some fellow get ahead in the world.'" Mr. Shimerda is proud that Antonia is a hard working farm-hand (final paragraph), and in lines 55 – 56 the narrator states: "I used to think of the tone in which poor Mr. Shimerda, who could say so little, yet managed to say so much when he exclaimed, "My Antonia!" The absolute pride Mr. Shimerda has in his daughter is evidenced by the enthusiasm he expresses when he simply cries out her name.

ANSWER EXPLANATIONS: SUPREME COURT OPINIONS (DUAL PASSAGE)

Question #1: (D)

➤ *Question Type:* Vocabulary-in-Context
Immediately eliminate two answers: choice (A) restates a primary meaning of the word that does not work in this sentence, and choice (E) has the opposite meaning of what is asked. Cover the word "measurably" and substitute the remaining three choices. Neither choice (B) nor (C) makes sense in the sentence; choice (D) is the best synonym in this context.

Question #2: (E)

➤ *Question Type:* Main Idea or Primary Purpose
This is a main idea question that is addressed throughout the passage, but the opening lines of the first paragraph and the final paragraph both summarize Justice White's position. Choices (A), (B), (C) and (D) can be eliminated because they do not reflect Justice White's objections to the death penalty. Choice (E) restates Justice White's reason for opposing the death penalty (summarized in lines 45 – 50).

Question #3: (D)

➤ *Question Type:* Modified Vocabulary-in-Context
Start with the second word in the phrase, "utility." Utility can refer to a gas or electric company or to something's usefulness. In this case, it is obviously the latter. The second words of the phrases in choices (A), (B) and (E) are not synonymous with "usefulness." Choice (C) would equate "morality" with "ideology." These words are not synonymous in any context. "Ethics" and "morality" are equivalent terms, so the answer is (D).

Question #4: (B)

➤ *Question Type:* Main Idea Variant
Four choices, (A), (C), (D) and (E), can be eliminated because they are not addressed by Justice White anywhere in the passage. Justice White's perspective is based upon the death penalty's role in the criminal justice system (lines 1 – 5), so choice (B) is the answer.

Question #5: (C)

➤ *Question Type:* Vocabulary-in-Context
Choices (A), (B) and (E) are all words that might be thought of in association with the actual act of execution. But the sentence is really saying that "the penalty is so infrequently imposed" that the threat of execution is adversely affected. According to Justice White, the problem with the death penalty stems from the rarity with which it is imposed. There is no mention made of inconsistency in its application, as stated in choice (D). The infrequent use of the death penalty lessens, or diminishes, its role in the criminal justice system. The answer is (C).

Question #6: (C)

➤ *Question Type:* Specific Detail
Choices (A), (B), (D) and (E) are all confirmed by statements in the passage. Choice (C) is refuted, as capital punishment is not considered a more effective deterrent than other punishments. Lines 23 – 28 state: "…a major goal of the criminal law – to deter others by punishing the convicted criminal – would not be substantially served where the penalty is so seldom invoked that it ceases to be the credible threat essential to influence the conduct of others."

Question #7: (A)

➤ *Question Type:* Main Idea Variant
Choices (B), (D) and (E) can be eliminated because they are not mentioned anywhere in the passage. While Justice Blackmun may in fact believe that the death penalty constitutes cruel and unusual punishment (choice (C)), that is not what causes the agony he experiences in these cases. Choice (A) explains the nature of Justice Blackmun's distress as stated in the first paragraph of the passage.

Question #8: (D)

➢ *Question Type:* Vocabulary-in-Context
Refer to the text and cover the word "buttressed" with your finger. Think of a synonym for the word as it appears in this sentence. The words that immediately come to mind are "supported" and "strengthened." Choices (A), (B), (C) and (E) are not synonymous substitutions, and all four choices can be eliminated. Choice (D), "reinforced," is an appropriate substitution for "buttressed."

Question #9: (E)

➢ *Question Type:* Specific Detail
Lines 54 – 63 of the second passage confirm choices (A), (B), (C) and (D). Justice Blackmun never states that he believes that the death penalty qualifies constitutionally as cruel and unusual punishment. The answer is (E).

Question #10: (C)

➢ *Question Type:* Modified Vocabulary-in-Context
The key phrase in the question sentence is "exercise executive clemency as Governor Rockefeller of Arkansas did." This phrase indicates that the answer choice must refer to the power of a state governor. Choices (A), (B), (D) and (E) do not refer to the power of a state governor. (C) is the only choice that refers to a state governor's authority with respect to the death penalty.

Question #11: (B)

➢ *Question Type:* Specific Detail
The "sole task for judges" is discussed in lines 82 – 85 of the second passage. These lines indicate that the judge's task has to do with evaluating the "constitutionality of legislation." Choices (A), (C) and (E) do not refer to this task. The Supreme Court does not "reshape" legislation (choice (D)). Its task is to "pass upon," or interpret the constitutionality of laws. This is stated in choice (B).

Question #12: (A)

➢ *Question Type:* Inference
Choice (A) is implied in line 94 in which Blackmun states: "I fear the court has overstepped." This leads to the conclusion that the Supreme Court should exercise less power than it does in certain instances. Choice (B) is not supported by the passage. The passage does not address specific crimes. Choice (C) is directly stated by the passage (see lines 73 – 77), so it does not represent an inference. Choice (D) is not supported by the passage. Lines 77 – 79 indicate that capital punishment should not be addressed by the judicial branch, but it does not refer to other Eighth Amendment issues. Choice (E) is directly stated by the passage (lines 62 – 66 and lines 67 – 69), so it cannot represent an inference.

Question #13: (E)

➢ *Question Type:* Comparison of Texts
Choice (A) is refuted by the passage. Justice White's opinion does not make reference to his personal feelings about the death penalty. Justice Blackmun's strong aversion to the death penalty occupies most of the first paragraph of Passage 2. Choice (B) is refuted by the passage. Neither justice believes that the death penalty serves a useful purpose in the criminal justice system. Choice (C) is not true. Justice White believes that murderers or rapists facing execution may, in fact, deserve this punishment (see lines 7 – 10 of Passage 1). Choice (D) can be eliminated because neither justice even mentions the Fourteenth Amendment of the Constitution. Choice (E) is confirmed by comparing the two passages. While Justice White's opinion is based upon the role of capital punishment in the criminal justice system, Justice Blackmun's opinion is based upon his belief that the Supreme Court has no authority in this matter.

VOCABULARY-IN-CONTEXT: ANSWERS

1. (D)   2. (C)   3. (D)   4. (E)   5. (E)   6. (C)
7. (C)   8. (D)   9. (D)   10. (D)

Critical Reading
Chapter 5

Sentence Completions

Strategies:

✔ **Sentence Completion Strategy #1:**

- **Understand the SAT's Instructions for Sentence Completion Questions**
- **Know How the Questions Will Look**
- **Manage Your Time Effectively in Answering Sentence Completion Items**

Sentence Completion items are sentences in which one or two blanks represent a missing word or words. Beneath the sentence are answer choices (A) – (E), each of which contain a possible word or pair of words to insert in the blank or blanks. Select the word or set of words that best suit the blanks to complete the sentence with clear and correct meaning.

Example:

1. The river does not flow ---- through the canyon; on the contrary, the white water rapids tumble swiftly over a succession of waterfalls.

    (A) inadvertently
    (B) sufficiently
    (C) lazily
    (D) regularly
    (E) predictably

The answer is (C), "lazily." The phrase "on the contrary" indicates that the sentence changes direction, and that the word that goes in the blank must contrast with the word "swiftly."

Sentence Completion items are usually found at the beginning of certain Critical Reading sections. **You should plan to spend no more than 40 seconds per question.**

✔ **Sentence Completion Strategy #2:**

- **Learn to Identify Continuation, Contrast, Example and Consequence Cues**

Consider these two "Sentence Completions:"

> I love my cousin, and _____.
> I love my cousin, but _____.

Here are some choices for completing the first sentence:

> I love my cousin, *and* he is a good role model.
> I love my cousin, *and* he is a loyal friend to me.

But what about the second sentence?

> I love my cousin, *but* sometimes he gets on my nerves.
> I love my cousin, *but* he can be very aloof.

Notice that the first part of each sentence differs by only one word: *and* is changed to *but*. This one small change is responsible for a change in the entire direction the sentence then takes.

CONTINUATION CUES: The word *and* is a continuation cue, indicating that what comes after it will be consistent with what was said before it:

(positive idea)	*(continuation cue)*	*(another positive idea)*
⇓	⇓	⇓
I love my cousin,	and	he is a good role model.

OR

(negative idea)	*(continuation cue)*	*(another negative idea)*
⇓	⇓	⇓
I find my cousin annoying,	and	he can be very ignorant.

CONTRAST CUES: The word *but* changes the direction (and tone of the sentence). What comes before the word *but* contradicts, or contrasts, that which follows:

(positive idea)	*(contrast cue)*	*(negative idea)*
⇓	⇓	⇓
I love my cousin,	but	sometimes he gets on my nerves.

OR

(negative idea)	*(contrast cue)*	*(positive idea)*
⇓	⇓	⇓
I find my cousin annoying,	but	he is actually very kind.

In Sentence Completions, continuation and contrast cues such as *and* and *but* are cues that indicate how different phrases in a sentence will relate to the other.

Continuation cues are words that <u>sustain</u> the sentence's tone and direction.
Contrast cues are words that <u>change</u> the sentence's tone and direction.

Important cue words are identified in the chart below. **Be sure to circle all cue words in Sentence Completion questions, as they are important clues in identifying the correct answer.**

IMPORTANT CUE WORDS FOUND IN SENTENCE COMPLETION QUESTIONS

CONTINUATION CUES	CONTRAST CUES	EXAMPLE CUES	CONSEQUENCE CUES
; (a semicolon), and, additionally, in addition to, furthermore, as well, also, moreover, besides	but, however, although, in spite of, conversely, on the contrary, nevertheless	such as, for example, for instance, a case in point, as evidenced by	due to, as a result, therefore, thus, so, consequently, hence, because, accordingly, in summary

---

✓ Sentence Completion Strategy #3:

• Know Whether the Blanks Require Positive or Negative Words

Many Sentence Completions blanks are filled with very polarized words – either positive or negative.

Compliment or Insult?

Consider the following Sentence Completion item:

> 2.   The King of Hamner was a(n) ---- and iniquitous tyrant who regularly exiled his enemies without justification.

Ask yourself: Is this king a good guy or a bad guy? He is clearly a bad guy because he is a "---- and iniquitous tyrant." *Iniquitous* means "characterized by wickedness." A *tyrant* is "a ruler who exercises absolute power oppressively or brutally." This sentence describes the king in negative terms. Whatever word goes in the blank will also describe him negatively, just as the words *iniquitous tyrant* do. Suppose that the following were the answer choices for this Sentence Completion:

> (A)   admirable
>
> (B)   exalted
>
> (C)   dilatory
>
> (D)   meticulous
>
> (E)   unscrupulous

Next to each answer choice:

➤   Put a (+) if the word is **positive**

➤   Put a (–) if the word is **negative**

➤   Put a (/) if the word is **neutral**

+	(A)	admirable	(means "deserving the highest esteem")
+	(B)	exalted	(means "raised in rank, power, or character")
–	(C)	dilatory	(means "characterized by procrastination")
/	(D)	meticulous	(means "marked by extreme or excessive care in the consideration or treatment of details")
–	(E)	unscrupulous	(means "lacking moral principle")

The two negative word choices are (C) and (E). (E) is the best choice because the king is not described as a procrastinator, but rather as lacking in morals or scruples when he unjustifiably exiles his enemies.

Practice Exercises: Positive or Negative

For each of the following sentences, decide if the word that fits in the blank is positive or negative.

1.   Often a ---- person, he surprisingly donates considerable sums to charity.
2.   Although many believe he is uncaring and detached, he is actually a(n) ---- president, truly interested in the plight of the less fortunate.
3.   The ---- but fair judge sentenced the man to life in prison.
4.   The toucan was completely ---- by the other birds in the aviary; they acted as if it wasn't even in their midst.
5.   The coach was considered a psychological genius, able to ---- a team that was formerly fragmented by the big egos of several players.

Answers:

1. –   (miserly)
2. +   (empathetic)
3. –   (harsh)
4. –   (ignored)
5. +   (unify)

✓ **Sentence Completion Strategy #4:**

• **Dealing with Double Blanks**

---

1.   **When two blanks are joined directly by continuation or contrast cues,** it is fairly easy to determine the nature of the words that will occupy the blanks. The chart below summarizes these instances:

SENTENCE COMPLETIONS:
WHEN TWO BLANKS ARE JOINED BY A WORD OR A SHORT PHRASE

Structure of the Sentence Completion	Examples	Words for the Blanks
Blanks are joined by continuation cue	---- and ----	The words will be **both positive or both negative,** or the words will be **synonym variants**
Blanks are joined by contrast cue	---- but ---- ---- rather than ----	**One** of the words will be **positive** and **one negative,** or the words will be **antonym variants**

2.   **Watch out for reversals!** Students are often drawn to answer choices in which the first word in the answer choice fits the second blank and the second word fits the first blank. The words in the correct answer choices must be presented in the right order.

3.   **Tackle the easier blank first.** Quickly decide which blank looks easier to fill, especially for long or complex Sentence Completion items. Consider the following question:

> 3.   From the quarterback's ---- record, one would easily conclude that he must have been a talented and ---- athlete.
>
> (A)   musical..philosophical
> (B)   statistical..capable
> (C)   gifted..past
> (D)   inconsistent..proficient
> (E)   compiled..healthy

The second blank looks easier to approach. It is part of the phrase a "talented and ---- athlete." Whatever goes in the blank will be a word that supports or is synonymous with the word *talented*. The choices that are consistent with the word *talented* are in (B), *capable*, and (D), *proficient*.

After the choices have been narrowed down for one of the blanks, eliminate all other choices. The correct answer choice must contain words that work for both blanks.

Now determine by substitution which word is better for the first blank.

> (B)   "the quarterback's <u>statistical</u> record" *or*
> (D)   "the quarterback's <u>inconsistent</u> record"

The quarterback would not be viewed as having been *talented* if he had posted an inconsistent record. The answer must be (B).

Note that there is a reversal in choice (C). The first word fits the second blank and the second word fits the first blank!

| ✓ **Sentence Completion Strategy #5:** |
| • **Identifying and Understanding Appositives** |

An appositive is a noun or noun phrase. If an appositive follows a comma, it usually defines or describes the noun immediately preceding the comma. The following sentence demonstrates the use of an appositive:

> *The most entertaining performers at the circus are acrobats, limber athletes who are able to contort their bodies to swing with ease from one trapeze to the next.*

In this sentence the phrase "limber athletes who are able to contort their bodies to swing with ease from one trapeze to the next" defines the word immediately preceding it, which is "acrobats."

Consider the following Sentence Completion:

4.   The senator was committed to the interests of her ----, the voters in her own state.

(A)   participants
(B)   political party
(C)   supporters
(D)   constituents
(E)   lobbyists

The word that goes in the blank is defined by "the voters in her own state." The answer is (D), *constituents*.

Be aware of all of the incorrect but attractive answer choices in this question. Choices (B), (C) and (E) all contain words that can be associated with politics or politicians, but they are not defined by the appositive phrase.

Now try these exercises. By examining the appositive, you should be able to take a good stab at a word that could fit in the blank.

Practice Exercises: Appositives

Based on the appositive that occurs after the blank, predict a word that could correctly occupy the blank.

1.   The investor's bank account continued its ----, an accumulation of interest that was never spent.
2.   The doctor prescribed a(n) ----, a medication used to treat a bacterial infection.
3.   He wanted to convert ----, those who doubted the very existence of God.
4.   The spy was accused of ----, the betrayal of his country.
5.   Mark Twain was Samuel Clemens' ----, an assumed name that he took from the terminology used to report river depth.
6.   Her husband thought she was a ----, a patient with whom doctors could never find anything truly wrong.
7.   They thought that the terrible earthquake was a(n) ----, a sign of things to come.
8.   The man practiced ----, the simultaneous marriage to several wives.
9.   The article addresses ----, the condition of being excessively overweight.
10.   The witness was accused of ----, the act of lying under oath.

Answers:
1. accrual
2. antibiotic
3. agnostics, unbelievers
4. treason
5. alias, pseudonym
6. hypochondriac
7. harbinger, omen
8. polygamy
9. obesity
10. perjury

> ✓ **Sentence Completion Strategy #6:**
>
> • **Listen Carefully to the Sound (Words That Sound Like What They Mean)**

Learn to use both your ears as well as your eyes to succeed at Sentence Completions. Certain words sound like what they mean. On Sentence Completion items with challenging vocabulary, you may be able to infer the meaning of some words by the way they sound.

Take for example, the word *disgusting*. If you were unfamiliar with the word *disgusting*, you could listen to how the word sounds. The word *disgusting* sounds awful – disgusting, in fact. Here are some equally unpleasant-sounding synonyms for the word *disgusting*:

> abhorrent
> odious
> repulsive
> revolting
> putrid
> sordid

Note that none of these words has a pleasant, euphonious sound. They all sound somewhat bad. If someone told you that something smelled putrid, you would not think of perfume – even if you had no idea what putrid meant. *Putrid* sounds like something that smells terrible.

Words that have positive meanings often have agreeable sounds. Consider the following pleasant-sounding synonyms of the word *calm*:

> serene
> composed
> demure
> sedate

Pronounce these words aloud. All of these words make smooth sounds. A word's soothing sound can help convey its definition.

Knowing that the sound of words can telegraph their meaning can help you considerably in filling in the blanks on Sentence Completions. If you determine that the word needed is positive or negative, but you do not know the meanings of the answer choices, the sound of the words may assist you.

5. The basketball player was exceptionally skilled, but he lacked the ---- needed to lead the team to victory.

    (A) volition
    (B) acrimony
    (C) turpitude
    (D) impudence
    (E) malfeasance

The blank should be occupied by a positive word, as it represents something that the basketball player "lacked" that was "needed to lead the team to victory."

Listen to the sound of each of the words in choices (B), (C), (D) and (E). Each of these words has a jarring or negative sound. Although you may not be sure that (A) is the best choice, the "sound" of each of the other choices does not seem right for the blank. *Volition* means "will." The basketball player did not have the will, or determination, to lead his team to victory.

Practice Exercises – Listening to the Sounds of Words

From the sound of each word, indicate whether it is a positive or negative word. Then attempt to define it:

1.   caustic:
2.   sublime:
3.   irascible:
4.   lethargic:
5.   mischievous:
6.   impudent:
7.   bellicose:
8.   trepidation:
9.   felicitous:
10.   equitable:

Answers:

1.   caustic (–): corrosive or acidic
2.   sublime (+): awe inspiring
3.   irascible (–): irritable or grumpy
4.   lethargic (–): sluggish or weary
5.   mischievous (–): ill behaved
6.   impudent (–): disrespectful
7.   bellicose (–): combative
8.   trepidation (–): apprehension
9.   felicitous (+): fortunate
10.   equitable (+): fair

IMPORTANT NOTE: You should not routinely rely purely on the "sound" of words to identify sentence completion answers, as this can be risky business. This strategy is intended for use on questions in which you are completely stumped by the vocabulary involved. A far better plan is to develop your SAT vocabulary with vocabulary flashcards, CDs or other study tools.

✔ **Sentence Completion Strategy #7:**

• **Look for Familiar Word Roots**

You may encounter answer choices that contain familiar word roots. Words that share the same root are related in meaning. If you identify a familiar root, you may know enough about a word to answer a question. Look at the following Sentence Completion:

6.   The ---- student could not help dozing off during the lecture.

    (A)   acerbic
    (B)   garrulous
    (C)   somnolent
    (D)   maniacal
    (E)   unfettered

Did you choose (C), *somnolent*? The root "som" should remind you of the word *insomnia*, the inability to sleep. *Somnolent* means "drowsy or sleepy."

✔ **Sentence Completion Strategy #8:**

• **Predict the Answer**

More so than any other question type on the SAT, Sentence Completions lend themselves to predicting the correct answer. When you first read a Sentence Completion, ask yourself what word or words might fit into the blanks. By anticipating the answer, you will be drawn to answer choices that match. You will also be less likely to be thrown off by reversals and attractors. As you read the following Sentence Completion, try to think of a word that would fit in the blank:

7.   The manufacturer's refusal to control industrial pollution ---- environmental activists.

A good prediction for the blank would be "bothered." Here are the answer choices:

    (A)   subdued
    (B)   awakened
    (C)   persuaded
    (D)   enraged
    (E)   confused

You should immediately see that the only possible synonym for "bothered" is choice (D), *enraged*. The word *enraged* is an extreme case of "bothered," but it sustains the meaning of the sentence. Forming an impression of the answer before actually reading the answer choices will help you move through the Sentence Completion items more quickly and more accurately.

✓ **Sentence Completion Strategy #9**

•   **Do Not Take A Creative Approach**

Often some very bright students who are excellent creative writers do not do well on Sentence Completion items. They are averse to what Sentence Completions actually measure: the ability to complete a sentence with a word or words that sustain its logical flow. Any words inserted in the blanks must be implied by something already stated in the sentence. **Sentence Completions are essentially a vocabulary test determining whether or not you can identify the missing word or words that are essentially defined by context clues within the sentence.**

The SAT does not reward creativity. Coming up with witty or original thoughts for Sentence Completions will not win you any style points. I once had in class a bright, gifted student who is a fine writer, crafting beautiful sentences replete with colorful adjectives and adverbs that added depth and meaning to her ideas. This is how she answered one Sentence Completion:

> 8.   The king, a visionary and ---- ruler, allowed the colonists to establish New
>   Marnwick, a territory thought to be opportune despite its ---- terrain.

"I think the answer is (B)," she announced. "*elderly* and *breathtaking*."

"'The king, a visionary and *elderly* ruler, allowed the colonists to establish New Marnwick, a territory thought to be opportune despite its *breathtaking* terrain,'" I read back.

"Yes!" she confirmed.

"What causes you to believe that the king is elderly?" I asked.

"What causes me to believe he is not?" she answered. "I visualize an old king, somewhat like King Lear but not as disturbed. He is old and about to die, so he wants to be known for establishing New Marnwick."

"And why is it that the terrain is breathtaking?" I continued.

"New Marnwick just sounds like the sort of place you would see advertised in a travel brochure. It would have to be breathtaking. I picture rocky cliffs above white sand beaches lined with palm trees," she responded.

"But New Marnwick is supposed to be opportune _despite_ something about the terrain," I pointed out.

"It is. Despite the beautiful cliffs, there will be successful fishing, and eventually tourism will take hold."

I took a deep breath and said, "You are reading too much into the sentence. You have to complete the sentence with words that, without question, finish the thought that the sentence is already presenting. You cannot add anything new to it. The right answer for this question is (C), *expansionist* and *rugged*. 'The king, a visionary and *expansionist* ruler, allowed the colonists to establish New Marnwick, a territory thought to be opportune despite its *rugged* terrain.'"

"So in other words, I am supposed to find the most trite and banal answer, one that in no way improves upon the sentence with any color or dimension," my student observed.

"Right!" I replied. "Trite and banal. Unoriginal. Complete the thought as stated. No new ideas. No color. No dimension."

"Fine," she agreed, "but it is a very boring approach."

"Boring but successful," I pointed out.

> ✓ **Sentence Completion Strategy #10**
>
> • **Re-read the Sentence with the Answer Choice to Make Certain it Sounds Correct**

Before you bubble in your answer selection, make sure you spend a moment to read the sentence back to yourself with the word or words from the answer choice in the blanks. This is a final check to make certain that you have not fallen for an attractor or a reversal. **If you read the sentence back to yourself with the blanks filled in and it does not sound quite right, that is your best clue that you have chosen the wrong answer!**

SENTENCE COMPLETIONS

CHAPTER 5 SUMMARY

1. **Spend about 40 seconds** on each Sentence Completion item.

2. **Be sure to circle all cue words in Sentence Completion questions,** as they are important clues in identifying the correct answer. *Continuation cues* are words that sustain the sentence's tone and direction. *Contrast cues* are words that change the sentence's tone and direction.

3. **Decide if the blank or blanks contain negative or positive words.** In each blank, put a (+) if the word is positive and a (–) if the word is negative. Then identify the answer choices with (+) and (–) signs or with (/) if the word is neutral. Match the blanks with the correct answer choice according to the "signs."

4. **If there are two blanks, watch out for reversals** – answer choices in which the first word in the answer choice fits the second blank and the second word fits the first blank.

5. **If there are two blanks, approach the easier blank first.** After the choices have been narrowed down for one of the blanks, eliminate all other choices.

6. If an *appositive* follows a comma, it defines or describes the noun (often times the blank in a Sentence Completion) immediately preceding the comma.

7. Learn to use both your ears as well as your eyes to succeed at Sentence Completions. **Certain words sound like what they mean.**

8.   **Knowing word roots, suffixes and prefixes** can assist you in determining the meaning of certain words.

9.   When you first read a Sentence Completion item, ask yourself what word or words might fit into the blank or blanks. **By anticipating the answer, you will be drawn to answer choices that are a match.**

10.   **The SAT does not reward creativity.** Sentence Completions are essentially a vocabulary test determining whether or not you can identify the missing word or words that are essentially defined by the remainder of the sentence's meaning.

11.   **Final check:** Before you bubble in your answer selection, read the sentence back to yourself with the word or words from the answer choice inserted in the blank or blanks.

SENTENCE COMPLETION PRACTICE

1. After a(n) ---- walking tour of Northern Italy, the travelers needed a truly restful vacation.

    (A) exciting
    (B) arduous
    (C) glimmering
    (D) scintillating
    (E) punctuated

2. The music performed at the concert was truly cacophonous, so ---- that members of the audience left the recital early.

    (A) discordant
    (B) muted
    (C) dizzying
    (D) repetitive
    (E) obtrusive

3. Applications to the university rose ---- after its ---- professor was awarded the Nobel Prize for his exhaustive research in quantum physics.

    (A) somewhat..quirky
    (B) little..famous
    (C) slightly..former
    (D) appreciably..esteemed
    (E) drastically..unknown

4. Although most meteors do not cause ---- destruction or injury when they fall to earth, some have been known to ---- homes and other small structures significantly.

    (A) irreparable..target
    (B) any..ruin
    (C) predictable..impact
    (D) widespread..pierce
    (E) considerable..damage

5. Despite the fact that most of the evidence presented was ----, the jury quickly ---- the defendant.

    (A) circumstantial..convicted
    (B) untrue..tried
    (C) factual..sentenced
    (D) unsubstantiated..acquitted
    (E) reasonable..judged

6. Because he constantly undermined the coach and questioned his teammates abilities, the entire team began to view its star player as more of a(n) ---- than a(n) ----.

    (A) dilemma..advantage
    (B) egotist..role model
    (C) eccentric..team player
    (D) instigator..arbitrator
    (E) liability..asset

7. Conventional medical therapies having failed, ---- but ---- new treatments were sought by the critically ill patient.

    (A) naturalistic..innovative
    (B) unproven..promising
    (C) unconfirmed..radical
    (D) rare..existent
    (E) experimental..solid

8. It was ---- that the prime minister was ultimately betrayed by the very ally he had once ---- implicitly.

    (A) unexplainable..regarded
    (B) expected..relied upon
    (C) shocking..befriended
    (D) forgotten..known
    (E) ironic..trusted

9.   The reform candidate's ---- absence at a corpora-
     tion's political fundraiser underscored his well-
     known opposition to the company's ongoing ----
     of labor laws.

(A) unplanned..support
(B) conspicuous..violations
(C) obvious..negotiation
(D) mere..awareness
(E) unexpected..disobedience

10. Although most viewers doubt the ---- of televi-
     sion psychics, they do believe that others possess
     ---- powers.

(A) veracity..specific
(B) reality..intuitive
(C) legitimacy..clairvoyant
(D) source..supernatural
(E) professionalism..authentic

SENTENCE COMPLETION ANSWER EXPLANATIONS

1. (B)

The travelers would have "needed a truly restful vacation" only if the "walking tour" had worn them out. The "walking tour" was difficult, or *arduous*.

2. (A)

The blank restates the meaning of "cacophonous." "Cacophonous" means inharmonious or *discordant*.

3. (D)

Deal with the second blank first. The word that fits in this blank must be positive because it describes someone who has won the Nobel Prize. The only answer choices with clearly positive second words are found in (B) *(famous)* and (D) *(esteemed)*. Now turn to the first blank. Because the professor has won the Nobel prize, applications to the university have probably risen substantially. The best remaining fit for the first blank is in choice (D), *(appreciably)*.

4. (E)

The contrast cue "although" indicates that the first half of the sentence will contradict the second half, making it possible to predict what sort of words will fit in the blanks. Here is a paraphrase: *Although meteors usually don't cause extensive destruction, they can harm structures significantly.* The best synonyms for "extensive" and "harm" are found in choice (E): *considerable* and *damage*.

5. (A)

The contrast cue "despite" indicates that the type of "evidence" is going to contrast with the jury's decision regarding the defendant. There are two choices: either the "evidence" was strong but nevertheless the jury set the defendant free, or the evidence was weak but the jury still found the defendant guilty. There is not a pair of words in an answer choice to fit the first possibility, but the second possibility is represented by choice (A). The lack of concrete evidence *(circumstantial)*

contrasted with the jury's decision when it *convicted*, or found guilty, the defendant.

6. (E)

The key phrase in this sentence actually contains both of the blanks: "more of a(n) ---- than a(n) ----" indicates that the word that goes in the first blank will be the opposite of the word in the second blank. The sentence indicates that the team now views its star player as a problem because of his attitude and behavior toward the coach and his teammates. The first blank will contain a word that is synonymous with "problematic" and the second blank will contain a word that means the opposite of "problematic." The best choice is (E): the athlete has become more of a *liability*, or negative factor, than an *asset*, or positive factor.

7. (B)

The key phrase in this sentence again contains both of the blanks: "---- but ----" indicates that the words in the blanks will have opposite meanings, or that one of the words will limit or qualify the other. In this sentence, try the positive/negative/neutral strategy, assigning values to the words presented in the answer choices, as the correct answer should contain a positive/negative or negative/positive word pair. Choice (A) is neutral/slightly positive. Choice (B) is negative/positive. Choice (C) is negative/slightly negative. Choice (D) is neutral/neutral. Choice (E) is neutral/slightly positive. Only choice (B) presents the contrast required.

8. (E)

Fill in the second blank first. Choices (A), (C) and (E) contain words for the second blank that could conceivably precede the word "implicitly." The word in the first blank must characterize the betrayal of the prime minister by a former ally. The word *ironic* best presents this unexpected development. The sentence is logically completed with the words from choice (E).

9. (B)

The key to this question are the words "reform candidate." Reform candidates are typically people who support fair labor laws. This gives us a clue about the second blank. The "reform candidate" probably missed the fundraiser because he disagrees with what the corporation does with respect to labor laws. Therefore, the two best choices for the second blank are (B) *(violations)* and (E) *(disobedience)*. The choices for the first blank then become (B) *(conspicuous)* and (E) *(unexpected)*. There was nothing unexpected about this absence – it was meant to "underscore" the candidate's opposition to the corporation's "violation of labor laws." The best answer is (B).

10. **(C)**

The contrast cue is "although." Use the fact that the first part of the sentence contrasts with the second part to predict words that can go in the blanks: *Although most viewers doubt the <u>validity</u> of television psychics, they do believe that others possess <u>psychic</u> powers.* The best synonyms for "validity" and "psychic" are found in choice (C), *legitimacy* and *clairvoyance*.

Writing
Chapter 1

Introduction & Grammar and Usage
(Identifying Sentence Errors)

Strategies:

1. Usage Question Instructions & How the Questions Will Look
2. Mini-Quiz for the Top Five Usage Errors
3. "Hear" the Error
4. Identify Subject and Verb Agreement Errors
5. Recognize Verb Tense Errors
6. Be Familiar with Irregular Verbs
7. Know Your Pronouns
8. Locate Misplaced Modifiers
9. Adverb or Adjective?
10. No Double Negatives
11. Comparative vs. Superlative Degree
12. Use Correct Prepositions
13. Eliminate Redundancy
14. Identify Word Choice and Diction Errors
15. Punctuation Guide

Tips & Strategies for Writing Skills Success
<u>on the SAT</u>

✔ **Writing – Usage Strategy #1:**
• **Know How the Questions Will Look**

The Writing section of the SAT features three different varieties of multiple-choice questions. Usage questions, also known as Identifying Sentence Errors, are the most prevalent. For these questions you must select the one underlined portion of the sentence that should be changed to make the sentence grammatically correct. You must assume that the parts of the sentence that are not underlined are correct and should not be changed. If there is no error, select choice (E).

Example:

1.   Tourists <u>napping</u> at the beach in the heat of the late <u>afternoon</u> as the sun
           (A)   (B)
     <u>set slowly</u> in the <u>western</u> sky. <u>No error</u>
         (C)   (D)   (E)

The answer to this question is (A) because this is a sentence fragment lacking a main verb. *Napping* should be used with a helping verb, e.g. *were napping.*

This chapter outlines all of the major grammatical or usage errors that you may encounter on the SAT's Usage or Identifying Sentence Error items. The next chapter addresses errors more commonly encountered in the second question type, Improving Sentences, but they may also come up in the Identifying Sentence Error questions. It is important to study both chapters with respect to both question types.

✔ **Writing – Usage Strategy #2:**
• **Be Acquainted with the Top Five Usage Errors**

The following five-question mini-quiz covers the top five Usage errors frequently missed by students. Take the quiz and then review the answer explanations.

(1)   <u>Regardless of</u> the members' individual talents, a fellowship of distinguished scientists always <u>work</u>
           (A)   (B)
     collaboratively and successfully during <u>its</u> annual convention <u>to advance</u> global research. <u>No error</u>
                                                    (C)   (D)   (E)

(2)   <u>Because</u> he had not been convinced that the girl would go <u>out on a date</u> with him, he <u>had asked</u> her
           (A)   (B)   (C)
     <u>to go out</u> with a group of their friends. <u>No error</u>
         (D)   (E)

(3)   Kryss's friend rented a jeep for <u>she and Jackie</u> so that the two of them <u>could go</u> surf and <u>explore</u> the best
                                                    (A)   (B)   (C)

            beaches <u>of</u> Costa Rica. <u>No error</u>
                        (D)   (E)

(4)   A successful college applicant <u>will make</u> a point <u>to get</u> good grades, do well <u>on</u> standardized tests, write
                                                          (A)   (B)   (C)

            an effective college entrance essay, and complete all of <u>their</u> assignments on time. <u>No error</u>
                                                                                    (D)   (E)

(5)   My nephew <u>noticed that</u> his performance <u>seemed to have caught</u> the attention of an agent in the audience
                            (A)   (B)

            and thought <u>that this</u> might favorably <u>effect</u> his career. <u>No error</u>
                              (C)   (D)   (E)

The following are the top five SAT Usage errors that are routinely overlooked by even the best students:

1.   Subject – verb agreement errors
2.   Verb tense errors *(compatible and corresponding tenses)*
3.   Pronoun case errors *(objective vs. nominative)*
4.   Pronoun-antecedent agreement errors
5.   Diction/word choice errors *(confused words or inappropriate word selection)*

Usage Quiz – Answer Explanations:

(1)   (B)
Subject – verb agreement error. Distancing the subject from its verb is the primary tactic used by test designers to create hard-to-find agreement errors. The subject of the sentence is *fellowship* (a singular, collective noun). The sentence incorrectly presents the plural verb *work*. The correct subject – verb form would be *fellowship works*. *(See Usage Strategy #4: Identify Subject and Verb Agreement Errors)*

(2)   (C)
Verb tense error. This sentence presents an incorrect double use of past perfect verb tenses. The past perfect verb *had asked* needs to be changed to the simple past tense *asked. (See Usage Strategy #5: Recognize Verb Tense Errors)*

(3)   (A)
Pronoun case error. Nominative case pronouns are used as subjects: *I, we, he, she, they.* Objective case pronouns are used as objects of prepositions, direct objects, or indirect objects: *me, us, him, her, them.* In the sentence in this exercise, the preposition *for* before *she and Jackie* dictates the use of an objective case pronoun. Therefore, *she and Jackie* should be replaced with *Jackie and her. (See Usage Strategy #7: Know Your Pronouns)*

(4)   (D)
Pronoun-antecedent agreement error. Agreement errors are a favorite among test designers, and this type employs the same "distancing tactic" that often creates subject – verb agreement errors. Note that the phrase *their assignments* is light years away from *applicant*, the subject of the sentence. The pronoun *their* is plural and does not agree with the singular antecedent *applicant*. Substitute *his or her* for *their. (See Usage Strategy #7: Know Your Pronouns)*

(5)   (D)

Word choice error. *Effect* can be used as a noun meaning "result" or as a verb meaning "to create an external result." The word *affect* is primarily used as a verb meaning "to influence" or "to create a reaction within." *Affect* is not typically used as a noun, except in the field of psychology in which it refers to a person's ability to respond emotionally. *Effect* should be replaced with *affect*: *...this might favorably affect* (or influence) *his career. (See Usage Strategy #14: Identify Word Choice and Diction Errors)*

Give yourself an "A" for effort! Taking this quiz may have shown you just how tricky SAT Usage questions can be. Take heart. This guide fully covers the above-illustrated errors as well as the test designers' other favorites. It also includes representative practice exercises that will help you to refine your abilities.

Competence and confidence build upon one another. Watch a young child practicing basketball free throws and you might say, "That child misses so often that he/she is just practicing mistakes." Eventually, however, more balls go in the hoop because the human brain has a marvelous way of recording successes even in a seeming sea of mistakes. In fact the greatest home run kings of baseball often hold the league record in strikeouts. Practice may not always make perfect...but perfection is seldom achieved without it. Let's get started!

✔ **Writing – Usage Strategy #3:**

• **"Hear" the Error**

Grammar is a piano I play by ear.

– Joan Didion

You have been listening to spoken English for quite a while. **When part of a sentence is not grammatically correct, you can often "hear" it – it just does not sound right.** While you cannot rely solely on this strategy, you can certainly make use of it on certain questions. You may not know the grammatical rule for the error, but you know that something is incorrect because part of the sentence sounds awkward. In the following sentence, you can probably "hear" that the verb tense sounds incorrect:

Yesterday after school, Seth had been eating a sandwich.

Something does not sound right with the verb phrase *had been eating*. The word *yesterday* indicates that a past tense verb should be used; *had been eating* should be replaced with *ate*:

Yesterday after school, Seth ate a sandwich.

The next example includes another error that you can "hear":

A discussion about the workers' desire of taking a longer lunch break will occur at today's executive meeting.

In this sentence, something sounds funny about the phrase *of taking*. This is a classic example in which a gerund is inappropriately used and should be replaced with an infinitive. The phrase *of taking* should be replaced with *to take*:

A discussion about the workers' desire to take a longer lunch break will occur at today's executive meeting.

Obviously many of the grammatical and usage errors on the SAT are not this easy to identify. However, whenever you do "hear" a grammatical error and you cannot find any other errors in the sentence, trust your instincts. If something in a sentence sounds wrong, it probably is wrong.

✓ Writing – Usage Strategy #4:

•   Identify Subject and Verb Agreement Errors

The following Usage question contains an error in subject – verb agreement:

2.   The original manuscript, <u>which is kept in</u> the library's special collections,
                            (A)
    <u>evidence</u> a historical <u>context lost</u> <u>through repeated</u> translations. <u>No error</u>
        (B)   (C)   (D)   (E)

The subject of this sentence, *manuscript*, does not agree with the verb, *evidence*. The answer is (B) because the word *evidence* should be replaced with *evidences*.

One of the top Usage errors found in SAT Writing questions has to do with subject – verb agreement. Singular subjects require singular verbs. Plural subjects require plural verbs:

The <u>subject</u> of the sentence <u>agrees</u> with its verb.
In this sentence, the subject *(subject)* is singular and the verb *(agrees)* is singular.

The <u>subjects</u> of sentences <u>agree</u> with their verbs.
In this sentence, the subject *(subjects)* is plural and the verb *(agree)* is plural.

Take a look at the following Identifying Sentence Errors item:

3.   The population of condors <u>along the coastal</u> regions <u>continue</u> to fall,
                                (A)   (B)
    but environmentalists <u>maintain that</u> they are not <u>in danger of extinction</u>.
                            (C)   (D)
    <u>No error</u>
    (E)

What do you think the subject of this sentence is? Here is a hint:

> **THE SUBJECT OF A SENTENCE CANNOT BE FOUND IN A**
>
> **PREPOSITIONAL PHRASE OR A DEPENDENT CLAUSE**
>
> Examples of prepositional phrases: *at the beach, under the table, over the hill*
>
> Examples of dependent clauses:
> *Before we go the store,...   Flying over the mountains,...*

The word *condors* is found in the prepositional phrase *of condors*. This prepositional phrase immediately follows the actual subject, which is *population*. The word *population* is a singular subject. It is a group (in this case, a group of *condors*) acting as a single unit. The verb *continue* fits a plural subject. Just listen to how it sounds if the subject is right next to the verb: *Population continue to fall.* No. That sounds goofy. It should be: *population continues to fall.* The error in the question is the verb *continue* which should be *continues*. So the answer is (B).

You might think that subject – verb agreement errors are easy to spot. You would be surprised how many students do not always catch them. Here are some general tips for identifying subject – verb agreement errors:

1.   Correctly identify the subject of the sentence; remember that the subject cannot be found in a prepositional phrase or in a dependent clause.

2.   Identify the verb. The verb is the action that the subject is taking.
IF THE VERB IS UNDERLINED AS A POSSIBLE ERROR CHOICE, PAY EXTRA ATTENTION TO THE POSSIBILITY OF A SUBJECT – VERB AGREEMENT ERROR.

3.   Is the subject singular and the verb in a plural form? Or vice versa? If so, you have found the error.

4.   Employ Usage Strategy #3 and listen carefully to how the sentence sounds. Does it sound like the subject matches the verb? Take note if you "hear" an error in subject – verb agreement.

CROSS OUT PREPOSITIONAL AND OTHER PHRASES THAT COME BETWEEN THE SUBJECT AND THE VERB

Often times phrases between the subject and the verb cloud subject – verb agreement. Get rid of this clutter! If you cross out these phrases, the sentence's skeleton will more directly reveal subject and verb mismatches. Here is an example:

> *The talent of the lion trainers and clowns (is/are) not fully appreciated by the audience.*

The prepositional phrase *of the lion trainers and clowns* falls between the subject *talent* and the verb choices *is/are*. If you cross out this phrase, the correct verb form becomes clear:

> The   *talent*   ~~*of the lion trainers and clowns*~~   *is*   not fully appreciated
> SUBJECT   (prepositional phrase)   VERB
> (SINGULAR)   (SINGULAR)
>
> *by the audience.*

PRACTICE EXERCISES: SUBJECT AND VERB AGREEMENT
(CROSS OUT INTERVENING PHRASES)

Cross out the phrase that comes between the subject and the verb choices. Then underline the subject and choose the appropriate verb.

1.   The diplomatic efforts of the mayor (goes/go) unrecognized.

2.   The summary of the various reports turned in by the committee members (is/are) helpful in developing a plan of action.

3.   Adrienne's concern about the possibility that her grandchildren's birthday presents had been mailed to wrong addresses (was/were) justified when the gifts ended up in Indonesia.

4.   The degree of toxins and other waste products (is/are) much higher than it used to be.

5.   The gymnastics scoring procedure used in the Olympic Games (has/have) changed considerably over the years.

Answers:

1.   The diplomatic <u>efforts</u> ~~of the mayor~~ (goes/<u>go</u>) unrecognized. *(Subject and verb are plural)*
           SUBJECT

2.   The <u>summary</u> ~~of the various reports turned in by the committee members~~ (<u>is</u>/are) helpful in developing a
           SUBJECT
       plan of action. *(Subject and verb are singular)*

3.   Adrienne's <u>concern</u> ~~about the possibility that her grandchildren's birthday presents had been mailed to~~
               SUBJECT
       ~~wrong addresses~~ (<u>was</u>/were) justified when the gifts ended up in Indonesia. *(Subject and verb are singular)*

4.   The <u>degree</u> ~~of toxins and other waste products~~ (<u>is</u>/are) much higher than it used to be. *(Subject and verb*
           SUBJECT
       are singular)

5.   The gymnastics scoring <u>procedure</u> ~~used in the Olympic games~~ (<u>has</u>/have) changed considerably over the
                       SUBJECT
       years. *(Subject and verb are singular)*

WHEN THE VERB COMES BEFORE THE SUBJECT

The following sentence is a passive construction, and the grammatical order we are accustomed to in sentences with active verbs is reversed. In this sentence, the subject, *trees*, follows the verb, *are*:

In front of the hotel are several beautiful palm trees.

You might have thought for a moment that the subject of this sentence is *hotel*. But *hotel* falls inside the prepositional phrase *in front of the hotel*, so it cannot be the subject. Change the order of the sentence, and the subject becomes clear:

Several beautiful palm trees are in front of the hotel.

In this sentence the subject, *trees*, precedes the verb, *are*.

If a sentence strikes you as "backwards" with the subject following the verb, take the following approach in analyzing subject – verb agreement:

1.	Find the verb and underline it. WHEN THE VERB PRECEDES THE SUBJECT, THE VERB IS OFTEN A PRESENT OR PAST TENSE FORM OF THE VERB "TO BE": *is, are, was, were.*

2.	Ask yourself who or what, exactly, is "doing" or "being" the verb. In the example above, what, exactly, *are*? Why, it is *trees* that *are*. It is not the *hotel* that *are*.

3.	Switch the order of the sentence. Place what you think is the subject before the verb and move the other verbiage after the verb.

4.	Be alert when compound subjects (e.g. "peaches and pears" or "Jason and Connor") follow verbs. With few exceptions, compound subjects require plural verbs.

PRACTICE EXERCISES: SUBJECT – VERB AGREEMENT
(VERB COMES BEFORE SUBJECT)

Try these exercises for practice. Underline the subject. Then choose the correct form of the verb.

1.	Where (is/are) the sausage and pineapple pizzas?

2.	On the museum's main floor (stands/stand) the statue from ancient Greece and the Egyptian artifacts.

3.	Along the bottom of the ocean (swims/swim) the stingray and his relatives.

4.	On top of the building (exists/exist) a helicopter pad and a windsock.

5.	Behind the fair's exhibits (was/were) the carousel.

Answers:

1.   Where (is/<u>are</u>) the sausage and pineapple <u>pizzas</u>?

2.   On the museum's main floor (stands/<u>stand</u>) the <u>statue</u> from ancient Greece <u>and the</u> Egyptian <u>artifacts</u>.

3.   Along the bottom of the ocean (swims/<u>swim</u>) the <u>stingray and his relatives</u>.

4.   On top of the building (exists/<u>exist</u>) a <u>helicopter pad and a windsock</u>.

5.   Behind the fair's exhibits (<u>was</u>/were) the <u>carousel</u>.

<u>INDEFINITE PRONOUNS AS SUBJECTS</u>

With few exceptions, indefinite pronouns require a definite verb form (singular or plural). Your mission is to memorize the chart below. The indefinite pronouns that end with *-body* or *-one* go with singular verbs, as do *each/either/neither*.

Indefinite Pronoun Operating as the Subject	Verb Agreement: Singular or Plural	Example
Anybody Everybody Somebody Nobody Anyone Everyone Someone No one Each Either Neither	*All Singular*	***Anybody*** at the school **knows** where the library is. ***Everybody*** **believes** it is true. ***Somebody*** **needs** to lead the group. ***Nobody*** **listens** to the boss. ***Anyone*** under twelve **gets** in free. ***Everyone*** in Spain **eats** dinner after 8:00 p.m. ***Someone*** down the street **sings** in the morning. ***No one*** in the dorm **sleeps** past noon. ***Each*** student **has** his own book. ***Either*** grocery store **accepts** coupons. ***Neither*** class **is** full.
Both Few Several Many	*All Plural*	***Both*** of the women **vote** in the second district. ***Few*** **build** model airplanes. ***Several*** of them **travel** together. ***Many*** **dislike** eggplant.
Any Some All Most None	*Can be Singular or Plural*	***Any*** of them **reads** well. (SINGULAR) ***Some*** **learn** to assemble children's toys. (PLURAL) ***All*** **follow** the example he sets. (PLURAL) ***Most*** **receive** good grades in math. (PLURAL) ***None*** of the team **plays** an entire game. (SINGULAR)

PRACTICE EXERCISES: SUBJECT – VERB AGREEMENT
(INDEFINITE PRONOUNS AS SUBJECTS)

Underline the indefinite pronoun that serves as the subject of the sentence. Then choose the correct verb form.

1.   Each of the students (rides/ride) the bus to and from school.

2.   Nobody from the various associations (votes/vote) in the annual election.

3.   After the lawn is watered, either of them (turns/turn) off the sprinklers.

4.   In order to find food, both schools of fish (scours/scour) the ocean floor.

5.   Due to concerns about pollution, few states (allows/allow) industrial plants to use certain chemicals.

Answers:

1.   <u>Each</u> of the students (<u>rides</u>/ride) the bus to and from school. *(SINGULAR)*

2.   <u>Nobody</u> from the various associations (<u>votes</u>/vote) in the annual election. *(SINGULAR)*

3.   After the lawn is watered, <u>either</u> of them (<u>turns</u>/turn) off the sprinklers. *(SINGULAR)*

4.   In order to find food, <u>both</u> schools of fish (scours/<u>scour</u>) the ocean floor. *(PLURAL)*

5.   Due to concerns about pollution, <u>few</u> states (allows/<u>allow</u>) industrial plants to use certain chemicals. *(PLURAL)*

"Either/or" and "Neither/nor" as Correlative Conjunctions

Correlative conjunctions are pairs of words used to link words, phrases or elements in a sentence. Correlative conjunction pairs include *either/or* and *neither/nor*.

When a compound subject is linked by a correlative conjunction pair, the subject closest to the verb determines whether the verb is singular or plural.

> *Examples: Neither* the teacher *nor* her students *were* present at the lecture.
> *Either* the senator *or* the representatives *have* the documents.

In both examples above, the subject closest to the verb is plural and a plural verb is used. If the subjects are switched so that the subject closest to the verb is singular, a singular verb is required. While this construction is grammatically correct, it can sound somewhat awkward.

> *Examples: Neither* the students *nor* their teacher *was* present at the lecture.
> *Either* the representatives *or* the senator *has* the documents.

The chart below provides further examples in which *either/or* and *neither/nor* are used as correlative conjunctions:

Description	Nouns or pronouns: Singular or Plural?	Verb: Singular or Plural?	Example
Subject contains two singular nouns/pronouns	Singular	Singular	*Either a bus or a van* **takes** the group to the amusement park. *Neither Leslye nor Holly* **has** received the fax yet. *Either a taco or a burrito* **comes** with the combination dinner.
Subject contains a singular noun/pronoun and a plural noun/pronoun (or vice versa)	One singular, one plural	Agrees with the closer subject noun or pronoun	*Either a tree or some flowers* **were** delivered to Dr. Li. *Neither the bricks nor the pathway* **matches** the rest of the yard.
Parts of the subject differ in person	Singular or plural	Agrees with the closer subject noun or pronoun	*Either Indi or I* **am** going to make the milkshakes. *Either Ryan or you* **are** next in line.

PRACTICE EXERCISES: SUBJECT – VERB AGREEMENT ("EITHER/OR" AND "NEITHER/NOR" AS CORRELATIVE CONJUNCTIONS)

Underline the correct verb for each sentence:

1. Neither the car nor the bicycles (is/are) in the garage.

2. Either the bananas or the mango (has/have) been added to the fruit salad.

3. After we eat breakfast together, either Maury or I (am/are) going to Santa Anita.

4. Either the teacher or the principal (meets/meet) with parents at the open house.

5. Neither the highway nor the side streets (leads/lead) to the wilderness area.

Answers:

1. Neither the car nor the bicycles (is/<u>are</u>) in the garage. *(PLURAL)*

2. Either the bananas or the mango (<u>has</u>/have) been added to the fruit salad. *(SINGULAR)*

3.   After we eat breakfast together, either Maury or I (<u>am</u>/are) going to Santa Anita. *(SINGULAR)*

4.   Either the teachers or the principal (<u>meets</u>/meet) with parents at the open house. *(SINGULAR)*

5.   Neither the highway nor the side streets (leads/<u>lead</u>) to the wilderness area. *(PLURAL)*

SUBJECT – VERB AGREEMENT: SPECIAL CASES

Special Subject-Verb Agreement Special Case #1:
The word "and" connects the subject parts

Description	Nouns or pronouns: Singular or Plural?	Verb: Singular or Plural?	Example
Compound subject in which each noun or pronoun is thought of as a separate entity	Singular or plural	Plural	*The oranges and the apple* **are** ripe. *She and Susie* usually **drive** to the retreat together. *The gorillas and the monkeys* **have** the best location at the zoo.
Compound subject type in which the nouns or pronouns act as a unit	Singular or plural	Singular	*"Peace and Freedom"* **is** their motto. *"The King and I"* **is** playing at the local theatre.

Special Subject-Verb Agreement Special Case #2:
Subjects that involve collective nouns or nouns that end in "*s*"

Description	Nouns or pronouns: Singular or Plural?	Verb: Singular or Plural?	Example
Collective nouns (*Examples:* team, board, committee, pack, herd, family, group)	Can be singular or plural, depending upon use	Singular or plural	The play's *cast* **performs** the dress rehearsal this evening. (Here *cast* is thought of as a single unit performing the play together.) The *cast* **are** rehearsing their lines in various locations backstage. (Here *cast* is thought of as various individual performers.)
Singular subjects that sound plural because they end in the letter *s*	Singular	Singular	*Corn fritters* **is** a popular food in some areas. *The running of the bulls* **is** a big event in Spain.

PRACTICE EXERCISES: SUBJECTS – VERB AGREEMENT
(SPECIAL CASES)

Underline the correct verb form in each of the following sentences:

1.   He and Susan often (flies/fly) to the publisher's convention together.

2.   The Trojans (is/are) a good football team.

3.   The committee (forms/form) an opinion after carefully considering the proposal.

4.   "Hannah and her Sisters" (was/were) a popular movie.

5.   Fried green tomatoes (is/are) still on the lunch menu.

Answers:

1.   He and Susan often (flies/<u>fly</u>) to the publisher's convention together. *(PLURAL)*

2.   The Trojans (<u>is</u>/are) a good football team. *(SINGULAR)*

3.   The committee (<u>forms</u>/form) an opinion after carefully considering the proposal. *(SINGULAR)*

4.   "Hannah and her Sisters" (<u>was</u>/were) a popular movie. *(SINGULAR)*

5.   Fried green tomatoes (<u>is</u>/are) still on the lunch menu. *(SINGULAR)*

✔ **Writing – Usage Strategy #5:**

• **Recognize Verb Tense Errors**

The following Usage question contains a verb tense error:

4.   <u>Before traveling</u> <u>abroad to Germany</u>, Helga <u>has been painting</u> a
          (A)   (B)   (C)
<u>unique new portrait</u> of her lovely daughter. <u>No error</u>
          (D)   (E)

The answer is (C) because the verb phrase *has been painting* is in the wrong tense. The word *has* should be replaced with *had* to correctly form the past perfect tense.

Verbs tell *what* is happening. The verb's tense tells us *when* it is that something takes place: past, present or future.

VERBS
PAST TENSES

Simple Past Tense	Past Progressive Tense	Past Perfect Tense
Action at a fixed time in the past.	(*"Progressive" refers to action in progress*) Action that happened in the past when something else also occurred.	(*"Perfect" refers to completed or perfected action*) Used to express an action that preceded another, both of which occurred in the past.
Clue: Usually ends in -*ed*.	**Clues: Verb form ends in -*ing*. Helping verbs *was* and *were*.**	**Clue: Helping verb *had*.**
I studied yesterday.	*I was studying when the phone rang.*	*I had studied for weeks before I took the test.*
(When? *Yesterday*.)	**(When? *When the phone rang*.)**	**(When? *For weeks before I took the test*.)**

PRESENT TENSES

Simple Present Tense	Present Progressive Tense	Present Perfect Tense
Action that is happening now or that could occur at any time.	Action that is happening in the immediate moment.	Ongoing past action, recurring past action, or action continuing from the past into the present.
Clue: Singular form is the same as the infinitive of the verb, e.g. *to study*.	**Clues: Verb form ends in -*ing*. Helping verbs *am*, *is* and *are*.**	**Clue: Helping verbs *has* and *have*.**
I study all the time. **(When? *All the time*.)**	*I am studying right now.* **(When? *Right now*.)**	*I have studied every morning this week.* **(When? *Every morning this week*.)**

FUTURE TENSES

Simple Future Tense	Future Progressive Tense	Future Perfect Tense
Action expected to take place in the future.	Action that will occur in the future while something else also occurs.	Used to express an action that will precede another action, both of which will occur in the future.
Clue: Helping verb *will*.	**Clues: Verb form ends in -*ing*. Helping verb phrase *will be*.**	**Clue: Helping verb phrase *will have*.**
I will study over the weekend.	*I will be studying during the game.*	*I will have studied before the final exam.*
(When? *Over the weekend*.)	**(When? *During the game*.)**	**(When? *Before the final exam*.)**

Verb Tense Error #1:
The Sentence Has One Verb or Verb Phrase,
But it is in the Wrong Tense

When part of a sentence refers to a certain time frame and the verb refers to a different time frame, the verb is in the wrong tense. These errors are easy to identify because sentences containing them usually sound wrong.

Example:

INCORRECT: Before her tenth birthday, Aundrey *has learned* her multiplication tables.

Here the verb phrase *has learned* sounds wrong. It is! Because one event occurred before another, the past perfect form *had learned* is required. *One more example*:

INCORRECT: Rebecca *will be practicing* the piano after dinner.

Will be practicing is the future progressive tense and should only be used to refer to an action that will occur in the future while something else is also taking place. In the sentence above, if the word *after* were replaced with the word *during*, the sentence would be correct. To change the verb form to fit the original sentence, use the simple future tense.

CORRECT: Rebecca *will practice* the piano after dinner.

PRACTICE: VERB TENSE ERRORS
(SENTENCE HAS ONE VERB)

First, double underline the "time-frame" word or phrase that dictates the correct verb tense. Then underline the incorrectly used verb or verb phrase. Finally, in the blank at the end of the sentence, write the correct verb or verb phrase.

1.   Since he was a teenager, George played the violin. _____

2.   Linda is completing planting the flowers next weekend. _____

3.   The librarian shelves the books right now. _____

4.   Uncle Jerry is listening carefully to the biochemist's presentation before he visited his laboratory. _____

5.   Civil War soldiers will have fought courageously for both the Union and the Confederacy. _____

Answers:

1.   <u>Since he was a teenager,</u> George <u>played</u> the violin. *has played*

2.   Linda <u>is completing</u> planting the flowers <u>next weekend</u>. *will complete*

3.   The librarian <u>shelves</u> the books <u>right now</u>. *is shelving*

4.   Uncle Jerry <u>is listening</u> carefully to the biochemist's presentation <u>before he visited his laboratory</u>. *had listened*

5.   <u>Civil War</u> soldiers <u>will have fought</u> courageously for both the Union and the Confederacy. *fought*

Verb Tense Error #2:
The Sentence Has Two Verbs or Verb Phrases,
And One is in the Wrong Tense

SAT Writing questions may involve sentences with two verbs or verb phrases. Often times, one of the verbs or verb phrases is used correctly, but the other one is not.

Case #1: The Actions Both Take Place at the Same Time and Require the Same Verb Tense

Example:

INCORRECT: They dove to the bottom of the pool and *retrieve* Nicole's necklace before it was dark.

In the sentence above, the action takes place in the past tense because it is happening *before it was dark*. The word *dove* is correctly cast in the past tense, but the word *retrieve* is incorrectly used in the present tense. The word *retrieve* should actually be *retrieved*:

CORRECT: They dove to the bottom of the pool and *retrieved* Nicole's necklace before it was dark.

Case #2: The Actions Take Place at Different Times in the Past, and One Requires the Perfect Tense

Example:

INCORRECT: Last night at the theatre, Tony and Mary Ann sat by people they *ate* lunch with earlier in the day.

In the sentence above, two actions are taking place in the past, but one precedes the other. In this case, eating lunch occurred before attending the theatre, and the past perfect tense should be used for the earlier action:

CORRECT: Last night at the theatre, Tony and Mary Ann sat by people they *had eaten* lunch with earlier in the day.

Case #3: The Actions Take Place in Two Different Time Frames (Past, Present or Future), So Two Different Verb Tenses are Required

Example:

INCORRECT: I think that the campaign *is* over by early October.

In the sentence above, *think* indicates a present tense action. However, the reference to the campaign being *over by early October* is a future action requiring a future rather than present tense verb form:

CORRECT: I think that the campaign *will be* over by early October.

PRACTICE EXERCISES: VERB TENSE ERRORS
(SENTENCE HAS TWO VERBS)

In the sentences below, the correct verb or verb phrase is emboldened. Draw a line through the incorrect verb or verb phrase and write the correct version in the blank at the end of the sentence.

1.   The choir **sang** songs that they practiced that afternoon. _____

2.   Scientists **believe** that medical technology advances in the future. _____

3.   Their grandparents frequently **drive** to the store and have gotten the chicken dinner special. _____

4.   Lisa had retrieved her e-mails after she **had returned** several phone calls. _____

5.   Scott **drove** to the court and will have filed the documents before the hearing yesterday. _____

Answers:

1.   The choir **sang** songs that they ~~practiced~~ that afternoon. *had practiced*

2.   Scientists **believe** that medical technology ~~advances~~ in the future. *will advance*

3.   Their grandparents frequently **drive** to the store and ~~have gotten~~ the chicken dinner special. *get*

4.   Lisa ~~had retrieved~~ her e-mails after she **had returned** several phone calls. *retrieved*

5.   Scott **drove** to the court and ~~will have filed~~ the documents before the hearing yesterday. *filed*

VERB TENSE TIPS

Verb Tense Tip #1:
For Sentences that begin with *If*, Use the Past Perfect Tense

Example:

INCORRECT: If Mike *would have* asked me, I would have picked him up at the airport.

In the sentence above, the first *would have* is used incorrectly. The past perfect tense should always be used in *if* clauses.

CORRECT: If Mike *had* asked me, I would have picked him up at the airport.

Verb Tense Tip #2:
True Statements are Always Expressed in the Present Tense

INCORRECT: Ancient Greeks knew that the planetary orbits *were* elliptical.

This statement incorrectly makes a statement of fact in the past tense: *orbits were elliptical*. Planetary orbits have always been and will always be elliptical. Because this is a statement of fact or truth, it should be stated in the present tense.

CORRECT: Ancient Greeks knew that planetary orbits *are* elliptical.

Verb Tense Tip #3:
The Tense of the Main Verb Dictates the Tense for Infinitives and Participles (Sequential Action)

Infinitives:

CORRECT: Chris was excited *to try* the new abalone appetizer.

The main verb *was* is in past tense and the infinitive *to try* is the in present tense; excitement preceded trying the new appetizer.

CORRECT: Susan is relieved *to have learned* of her turtle's recovery.

The main verb *is* is in the present tense; the infinitive *to have learned* is in the past perfect tense; the learning of the recovery preceded her relief about it.

Participles:

CORRECT: *Having danced* late into the evening, the couple did not arrive home until after midnight.

The dancing occurs before the couple arrives home, so the perfect participle form *having danced* is used.

CORRECT: *Running* down the beach, Austin saw many of his friends.

Austin sees his friends as he runs, so the present participle *running* is used.

PRACTICE EXERCISES: VERB TENSE ERRORS
(APPLY VERB TENSE "TIPS")

Choose the correct verb form in each of the following sentences:

1.   If Norma (had/would have) turned on the light, she would have seen Siegfried sleeping.

2.   Newton proved that the laws of gravity (apply/applied) to all objects.

3.   (Teaching/Having taught) many classes about Shakespeare, the professor knew which plays students enjoyed the most.

4.   Anthony was eager to (tour/have toured) all of England's former colonies.

5.   While (cleaning/having cleaned) the house, we found Abigail's missing earmuffs.

Answers:

1.   had

2.   apply

3.   Having taught

4.   tour

5.   cleaning

✓ Writing – Usage Strategy #6:

- **Be Familiar with Irregular Verbs**
- **Do Not Confuse the Simple Past Tense with Past Participle Forms**

The following Usage question presents an error in the past participle form of the verb:

5. <u>Despite</u> her demanding schedule, Dawn <u>had awoke</u> <u>early at the hotel</u> so
   (A)   (B)   (C)
     that she could visit the new factory <u>site</u> with her employees. <u>No error</u>
                                    (D)   (E)

The simple past tense form of the verb *to awake* is *awoke*, but the past participle is *awakened*. Choice (B) is incorrect and should read *had awakened*.

In regular verbs, the simple past tense and the past participle are both formed by adding *-ed* to the infinitive form of a verb:

Present tense:	Mary *listens* to the radio every day.
Simple past tense:	Mary *listened* to the radio yesterday.
Past perfect tense: **(contains participle)**	Once she *had listened* to the radio reports, Mary went to the hardware store and bought storm shutters.
Present perfect tense: **(contains participle)**	Mary *has listened* to the radio every morning since the storm began.

The past and present perfect tenses combine the helping verbs *had*, *has* or *have* with the participle. Confusion arises when irregular verbs do not follow the standard pattern for forming past tense verb and participle forms. SAT Usage questions present errors in which the simple past tense is substituted for the participle or vice versa.

Example:

INCORRECT: Dixon *had came* just in time to dismantle the electronic device.

(This sentence incorrectly uses the helping verb *had* with the simple past tense *came* instead of the participle.)

CORRECT: Dixon *had come* just in time to dismantle the electronic device.

Make sure that you are familiar with the following irregular verbs:

Irregular Verb Triples: All Three Forms are The Same

Infinitive	Simple Past Tense	Participle
burst	burst	burst
put	put	put
set	set	set
shut	shut	shut

Irregular Verb Doubles: Two Forms are the Same
(Same Simple Past Tense & Participle)

Infinitive	Simple Past Tense	Participle
bring	brought	brought
hang	hung	hung
lay	laid	laid
lead	led	led
shine	shone	shone
sit	sat	sat
sting	stung	stung

Irregular Verbs: No Forms are the Same
The past tense usually includes a "long *o*" as a vowel and the participle ends in *-en* or *-ened*:

Infinitive	Simple Past Tense	Participle
awake	awoke	awakened
bid	bade	bidden
break	broke	broken
choose	chose	chosen
rise	rose	risen

The present tense ends in *-in*, *-ing* or *-im*; change the letter *i* to *a* to form the past tense or to *u* to form the participle:

begin	began	begun
ring	rang	rung
spring	sprang	sprung
swim	swam	swum

Miscellaneous:

bear	bore	borne
come	came	come
lie	lay	lain
tear	tore	torn
dive	dived or dove	dived
shrink	shrank or shrunk	shrunk or shrunken
spit	spit or spat	spit or spat
strive	strove or strived	striven or strived

Note: *Burn, dream* and *dwell* can all have regular past tense and participles with normal *-ed* ending or irregular *-t* ending (e.g. *burn/burnt/burnt*).

There are many other irregular participle forms; the chart on the preceding page is intended to provide an overview of some of those most commonly encountered.

✓ **Writing – Usage Strategy #7:**

• **Know Your Pronouns**

The Usage item that follows contains a classic pronoun error:

6. The trip that <u>had been planned</u> for <u>my husband and I</u> included many
               (A)   (B)
    ports of call, and we thoroughly enjoyed <u>extensive exposure</u> to
                                        (C))
    <u>many different cultures</u>. <u>No error</u>
        (D)   (E)

The phrase in choice (B) serves as the object of the preposition *for*, so the objective case pronoun *me* should be used instead of *I*. Choice (B) should read *my husband and me*.

Pronouns are words used to replace nouns. There are two main cases of pronouns, "nominative case" and "objective case." In the following sentence, there is one pronoun representing each case:

I sent the letter to her.

In this sentence, the word *I* is a nominative case pronoun and the word *her* is an objective case pronoun.

Nominative (or subjective) case pronouns are usually found in the subject of the sentence or in the sentence's predicate nominative. When they act as the subject, they perform the verb's action. In the above sentence, *I* is a nominative case pronoun and is also the subject of the sentence; it is *I* that performed the action of sending the letter.

Objective case pronouns usually follow prepositions and often function as direct or indirect objects. These pronouns are usually the recipients or objects of actions. In the sentence above, *her* is an indirect object receiving the direct object, which is the *letter*.

Pronoun Chart

	Nominative Case	**Objective Case**
1ST PERSON SINGULAR/PLURAL	I, we	me, us
2ND PERSON SINGULAR/PLURAL	you, you	you, you
3RD PERSON SINGULAR/PLURAL	he/she, they	him/her, them

The "I/Me" Method for Identifying Pronoun Mistakes

Use the "I/me" test to determine which kind of pronoun to use (objective case or nominative case):

1.   Replace the pronoun in question with the word "me."
2.   If the sentence sounds all right with the substitution of "me," use the appropriate objective case equivalent of "me" (*me, us, you, him, her* or *them*).
3.   If the sentence does not sound correct with the substitution of "me," try substituting the pronoun with the word "I." The sentence should now sound right with "I," so use the appropriate nominative case equivalent of "I" (*I, we, you, he, she* or *they*).

Example:

> The league officials requested that (he/him) and his associates return the photos
> to Derek and (she/her).

Substitute "me" in place of the first pronoun choice and the words coupled with the pronoun (*and his associates*):

> The league officials requested that *me* return the photos....

That sounds wrong. Now we will try substituting "I":

> The league officials requested that *I* return the photos...

That phrase sounds right, indicating that a nominative case pronoun choice is needed. The pronoun here should be *he*.

Now substitute "me" in place of the second pronoun phrase, "(she/her)":

> ...return the photos to *me*.

That sounds fine, so the objective case pronoun *her* is required here. The correct sentence is:

> The league officials requested that *he* and his associates return the photos to
> Derek and *her*.

TIPS FOR CHOOSING THE CORRECT PRONOUN

Pronoun Choice Tip #1: Pronouns Found in the Same Phrase Must be of the Same Case

In a given phrase, two pronouns both must be either nominative case or objective case pronouns. *Example:*

Use *"he and I"*   **not**   *"him and I"* or *"he and me"*

Use *"her and us"*   **not**   *"she and us"* or *"her and we"*

Pronoun Choice Tip #2: For Comparisons, Always Use Nominative Case Pronouns

INCORRECT: I type faster than *her*.
                (*her* is an objective case pronoun and is used incorrectly)

CORRECT: I type faster than *she* (does).
                (*she* is a nominative case pronoun and is used correctly)

PRACTICE EXERCISES: PRONOUN CHOICE

In the sentences below, choose the correct pronoun in each set of parentheses:

1.   (She/her) and (I/me) went to the grocery store for (he/him).

2.   (They/them) and their cousins came to get (we/us) at the airport at midnight.

3.   (She/her) and three other students gave their concert tickets to (he/him) and (me/I).

4.   (She/her) and (he/him) invited my niece and (I/me) to a Halloween party.

5.   (We/us) and our other teammates are planning to beat (they/them) in the upcoming tournament.

6.   My partner and (me/I) will be traveling to Monaco after passports are issued to (she/her) and (I/me).

7.   (They/them) and (we/us) agree that no report will be filed if (they/them) return the missing items to (he/him) and (I/me).

8.   (She/her), (he/him) and (I/me) will not leave town until (they/them) confirm that there are hotel reservations for (she/her) and (I/me).

9.   (They/them) ask my roommate and (I/me) to work overtime when (he/him) and (she/her) expect a lot of extra customers.

10.   The committee questioned (she/her) and (I/me) for hours before (they/them) dismissed (we/us).

Answers:

1.   <u>She</u> and <u>I</u> went to the grocery store for <u>him</u>.

2.   <u>They</u> and their cousins came to get <u>us</u> at the airport at midnight.

3.   <u>She</u> and three other students gave their concert tickets to <u>him</u> and <u>me</u>.

4.   <u>She</u> and <u>he</u> invited my niece and <u>me</u> to a Halloween party.

5.   <u>We</u> and our other teammates are planning to beat <u>them</u> in the upcoming tournament.

6.   My partner and <u>I</u> will be traveling to Monaco after passports are issued to <u>her</u> and <u>me</u>.

7.   <u>They</u> and <u>we</u> agree that no report will be filed if <u>they</u> return the missing items to <u>him</u> and <u>me</u>.

8.   <u>She</u>, <u>he</u> and <u>I</u> will not leave town until <u>they</u> confirm that there are hotel reservations for <u>her</u> and <u>me</u>.

9.   <u>They</u> ask my roommate and <u>me</u> to work overtime when <u>he</u> and <u>she</u> expect a lot of extra customers.

10.   The committee questioned <u>her</u> and <u>me</u> for hours before <u>they</u> dismissed <u>us.</u>

PRONOUN REFERENCE ERRORS

Pronouns often refer to some other noun or noun phrase in the sentence called an "antecedent." The pronoun is used instead of simply repeating the antecedent. *Example:*

Violette buys collectibles at every estate sale she visits.

In the sentence above, the pronoun *she* is used in place of *Violette*. *Violette* is the antecedent correctly referred to and replaced by the singular, personal pronoun *she*.

Pronoun Reference Error #1:
The Antecedent is Ambiguous (Two or More Possible Antecedents)

In some sentences, there is more than one noun or noun phrase that could be serving as the antecedent for a pronoun. These sentences can be fixed in two ways:

1.   Replace the pronoun with the actual noun or noun phrase. This can make the sentence sound repetitive and awkward, but sometimes it is the only solution.

2.   Re-work the sentence so any pronoun reference to an antecedent is clear.

Example:

VAGUE: Cheryll gave her sister a book she had read.

Who is it that read the book? Cheryll or her sister? The pronoun *she* is vague because we do not know if the antecedent referred to is *Cheryll* or *her sister*. Here are two revisions of the sentence following the repair rules stated above:

CLEAR: Cheryll gave her sister a book that Cheryll had read.

CLEAR: Cheryll gave a book she had read to her sister.

Here is another example:

VAGUE: Doreen and Emily agreed that she should look for her at the petting zoo.

We have no idea who should look for whom. The pronoun *she* could be referring to either Doreen or Emily, as could the pronoun *her*. In this case, because there are two pronouns, it is best to use the actual names of the people instead of pronoun substitutes.

CLEAR: Doreen and Emily agreed that Doreen should look for Emily at the petting zoo.

Pronoun Reference Error #2:
Missing Antecedent (No Specific Antecedent Exists)

In every day speaking, we frequently say and hear sentences such as the following:

INCORRECT: On the 7:00 news, they said it would rain tomorrow.

They probably refers to television weathermen or newscasters – but the sentence does not really specify who exactly *they* are. There is no stated antecedent that *they* actually refers to. Because the reference is implied rather than stated, it is grammatically incorrect. This sentence is most easily fixed by replacing *they* with a noun or noun phrase.

CORRECT: On the 7:00 news, the weather reporter said it would rain tomorrow.

Here is another example:

INCORRECT: During Roy's trip abroad, he photographed famous landmarks.

In this sentence, there is no antecedent for the pronoun *he*. We are probably meant to believe that *he* refers to *Roy*, but this is not clear. **Possessive adjectives cannot be used as antecedents for pronouns.** *Roy's* is not the same as *Roy*. To correct this sentence, switch the noun and the pronoun; the pronoun will change to the possessive form *his*.

CORRECT: During his trip abroad, Roy photographed famous landmarks.

Pronoun Reference Error #3:
The Antecedent Cannot Be Identified (A Specific Noun or Noun Phrase Acting as the Antecedent for a Relative Pronoun Cannot Be Pinpointed)

Relative pronouns include the following: *who, whom, whose, which* and *that*
Relative pronouns can create their own special confusion by referring to too many things (multiple item antecedents) or to a concept that is too broad in nature. *Example:*

INCORRECT: During our summer vacations at Bear Lake, we water ski, hike, swim and stay up late, which makes the trip a lot of fun.

What, exactly, makes the trip a lot of fun? Because all of things mentioned contribute to the fun, the sentence should be modified as follows:

CORRECT: During our summer vacations at Bear Lake, we water ski, hike, swim and stay up late, *all of which* make the trip a lot of fun.

✓ **Writing – Usage Strategy #8:**

• **Locate Misplaced Modifiers**

Can you spot the misplaced modifier in this Usage question?

7.   <u>To conclude</u> a <u>stirring outdoor ceremony</u>, ice statuettes <u>were presented</u> to
        (A)   (B)   (C)
      the guests <u>requiring immediate refrigeration</u>. <u>No error</u>
                        (D)   (E)

This sentence makes it sound as if the guests are in need of *immediate refrigeration*. To correct the sentence, the modifier in choice (D) should be placed right after the phrase *ice statuettes*.

Modifiers are words or phrases that are used to describe, or modify, another part of the sentence. There are two ways that modifiers are used incorrectly.

Modifier Error Type #1:
The Modifier is not in the Right Place in the Sentence (Misplaced Modifier)

INCORRECT: The store gave coupons to its customers that will expire at the end of the month.

The modifier is the phrase *that will expire at the end of the month*. The phrase is obviously meant to refer to the coupons, but it sounds as if it is the customers that will soon expire. To fix this type of error, the modifier must be placed as near as possible to the word or words modified, in this case the word *coupons*.

CORRECT: The store gave coupons that will expire at the end of the month to its customers.

Here is one more example:

INCORRECT: An article was written about the kidnapping by the reporter.

In this sentence, it sounds as if it is the reporter who has kidnapped someone. The modifier *by the reporter* should be moved next to the word modified, in this case *article*.

CORRECT: An article was written by the reporter about the kidnapping.

The following active construction is actually better:

CORRECT: The reporter wrote an article about the kidnapping.

A specific type of misplaced modifier involves **limiting modifiers,** or words that mean "almost." Limiting modifiers include the following: *almost, only, practically, barely, just, merely, hardly, scarcely, virtually, all but,* and *nearly*.

Example:

INCORRECT: The children *almost drank* all of the fruit punch.

The placement of the word *almost* in this sentence makes it seem as if they did not quite begin drinking the fruit punch. Limiting modifiers need to be placed after the verbs they modify to indicate the degree of the action that has been completed. In this case, the word *almost* must follow the word *drank*.

CORRECT: The children *drank almost* all of the fruit punch.

There! Now it is clear that there is not much fruit punch left because they *drank almost all* of it.

***Always place limiting modifiers immediately
in front of the word to be limited or modified.***

Modifier Error Type #2:
There is no Specific Word for the Modifier to Modify (Dangling Modifiers)

Example:

INCORRECT: While camping in the mountains, squirrels ate the trail mix.

This sentence makes it sound as if the squirrels were the ones who were camping. The modifier *while camping in the mountains* is meant to refer to those who are truly camping, not the squirrels. **The correct noun to be modified is completely missing.** To fix this error type, add the necessary noun or pronouns to be modified and revise the rest of the sentence as needed:

CORRECT: While the boys were camping in the mountains, squirrels ate their trail mix.

or

CORRECT: While camping in the mountains, the boys slept as squirrels ate their trail mix.

Dangling modifiers are usually found at the beginning or end of the sentence. They are usually one of the following:

➢ A verbal phrase with nothing to modify. *(A verbal phrase contains a verb form with an -ing ending)*

➢ A clause in which the subject and verb are omitted.

There are two ways to fix a sentence containing a dangling modifier:

1.   Turn the verbal phrase into a clause containing the sentence's subject and replace the verbal with a verb.

2.   Place the appropriate noun or pronoun immediately after the comma that follows the verbal phrase.

The following sentence contains a dangling modifier:

Noticing that the track was slippery, the race was postponed.

It was not the *race* that noticed that *the track was slippery*. This sentence is revised as follows according to the two methods identified above:

1.   Because the officials noticed that the track was slippery, the race was postponed.
2.   Noticing that the track was slippery, the officials postponed the race.

PRACTICE EXERCISES: MISPLACED MODIFIERS

The following sentences contain misplaced or dangling modifiers. Re-write them so that the modifiers are correctly used.

1.   Kathy left the magazine at the job site that she had been reading.

_____

2.   After eating lunch in the park, the tour bus proceeded to the museum.

_____

3.   Flying over the Rockies, snow was seen everywhere.

_____

4.   A speech was given about organized crime by the politician.

_____

5.   Ella gave bread to the peacocks with the crust removed.

_____

Answers:

1.   Kathy left the magazine she had been reading at the job site.

2.   After they ate lunch in the park, the tour bus took them to a museum. *or*
       After eating lunch in the park, they continued on the tour bus to the museum.

3.   Flying over the Rockies, we/they saw snow everywhere.

4.   A speech was given by the politician about organized crime.
       Or turn the sentence into an active construction (preferred):
       The politician gave a speech about organized crime.

5.   Ella gave the peacocks bread with the crust removed.

✔ **Writing – Usage Strategy #9:**
• **Use Adverbs and Adjectives Correctly**

Usage questions may present errors in which adverbs are incorrectly substituted for adjectives (or vice versa).

8.   Although environmental agencies <u>have insisted</u> that the industrial plant
                                           (A)
     <u>institute anti-pollution measures</u>, the air near the plant <u>continues to smell</u>
                        (B)   (C)
     <u>badly</u>. <u>No error</u>
      (D)   (E)

The verb *smell* is a linking verb that cannot be modified by an adverb. The word *badly* in choice (D) should be replaced with the word *bad*.

Adverbs modify active verbs. Verbs tell *what* action occurs. The verb tense tells *when* the action occurs. Adverbs modify verbs by telling *how, where* or *more specifically when* the action is taking place.

Example:

INCORRECT: Joshua ran quick. (Quick is an adjective, not an adverb)

CORRECT: Joshua ran *quickly*.

In the sentence above, the adverb *quickly* modifies the verb *run*. Most adverbs that modify verbs end in *-ly*.

Adverbs do not modify passive or linking verbs. Linking verbs (such as *feel, appear, smell, taste, seem, grow, become, stay, remain* and forms of the verb *to be*) cannot be modified by adverbs. (Note: If these verbs act as active rather than passive or linking verbs, then they can be modified by adverbs.)

Example:

INCORRECT: Leone remained calmly in the waiting room.

(*Calmly* is an adverb that cannot be used to modify *remain*, a linking verb.)

CORRECT: Leone remained *calm* in the waiting room.

(*Calm* is an adjective describing how *Leone* is.)

Good or Well?

Good is an adjective. For example, one does not *sleep good* or *swim good* – one *sleeps well* or *swims well*. When *well* is used as an adjective, it refers to a state of health. When the word *well* is not used to refer to physical health, it functions as an adverb. *Example:* "He played *well* in the championship game."

INCORRECT: Michael did good on the test.

(An adverb, *well*, not the adjective *good*, is required to modify the verb *did*.)

CORRECT: Michael did *well* on the test.

Here is another example:

INCORRECT: After she had surgery, Ann was feeling good, so Sandy took her to the family barbecue.

CORRECT: After she had surgery, Ann was feeling *well*, so Sandy took her to the family barbecue.

(In this case, *feel* is an active rather than a passive verb because it is associated with how the subject actually feels physically. The adjective *good* is incorrectly used; the adverb *well* is required to modify the active verb *feel*.)

**Feeling *good* refers to positive spirits or attitude;
feeling *well* has to do with a positive state of physical health.**

Bad or Badly?

When describing how someone feels psychologically or emotionally, use the adjective form: *He feels bad.*

He feels badly would mean that he lacks sensation, as if a part of his body were numb. To indicate a negative state of physical health (the opposite of *well*), use the following construction: *He feels poorly.*

INCORRECT: Julia felt badly when the dog bit Stuart.

(*Felt* is used here as a passive verb, so the adverb *badly* cannot be used.)

CORRECT: Julia felt *bad* when the dog bit Stuart.

PRACTICE EXERCISES: ADVERB VS. ADJECTIVE

Choose the correct adjective or adverb in each sentence.

1.   The cabbage soup tastes (terrible/terribly).

2.   Dr. Rosenquist grew (excited/excitedly) when the X-rays supported his diagnosis.

3.   The choir performed (bad/badly) without the orchestra.

4.   Joe Montana played (good/well) in four different Super Bowls.

5.   After he was moved to another stable, Lee's horse seemed (different/differently) to Cam.

Answers:

1.   terrible

2.   excited

3.   badly

4.   well

5.   different

✓ Writing – Usage Strategy #10:

* **Eliminate Double Negatives**

Can you "hear" the double negative error in the following Usage question?

> 9.   The director <u>of the marching band</u> was <u>quite surprised</u> to learn that hardly
>   (A)   (B)
>   <u>none of the drummers</u> wanted <u>to participate</u> in the local parade. <u>No error</u>
>   (C)   (D)   (E)

The double negative phrase is *hardly none*. The word *none* in choice (C) should be changed to the word *any*.

"Double negative" errors occur when two words derived from or related to the word *no* are found in the same sentence. These errors can be corrected in two different ways:

1. Eliminate one of the negative words entirely. *(This works only in certain cases.)*

2. Change one of the negative words to its positive equivalent (for example, change *nobody* to *anybody*). *(This works in all cases.)*

After you have repaired a sentence containing a double negative error, be sure to read it over to make certain that it sounds grammatically correct.

For the purposes of identifying double negative errors, the following are considered negative words:

Variations of the word "no"
not, none, nobody, nothing, never

Adverbs that mean "almost none"
scarcely, hardly, barely

Double negatives also occur when the words *but* or *only* follow another negative word:
can't help but, couldn't help but, hasn't only, haven't only, hasn't but, haven't but

Example:

INCORRECT: Hardly nobody came to class today.

CORRECT: Hardly anybody came to class today. *or*
                       Practically nobody came to class today.

   For the purposes of identifying double negative errors, negative prefixes do not make words negative.
Words with prefixes such as *im-*, *in-*, and *un-* can be used correctly with the word *not* or other negative words.

Example:

CORRECT: The lab results are not unimportant.

(The negative words cancel out. This sentence actually means that the lab results are fairly important.)

Although the words *neither* and *nor* both sound like negative words, they belong together and do not create double negative errors when found in the same sentence.

Example:

CORRECT: Neither Irina nor Katya can be fully trusted.

PRACTICE EXERCISES: DOUBLE NEGATIVES

Re-write each sentence below, correcting the double negative errors.

1.   The circus doesn't have no trapeze act.

         _____.

2.   Paula couldn't help but tell Marilyn the good news.

         _____.

3.   Elizabeth hardly never drives her husband's car to work.

         _____.

4.   Sandi hasn't only a week to file the tax returns for John.

_____.

5.   Scarcely none of the Lakers' players have ever experienced a losing season.

_____.

Answers:

1.   The circus doesn't have a trapeze act. *or*
     The circus has no trapeze act.

2.   Paula couldn't help telling Marilyn the good news.

3.   Elizabeth hardly ever drives her husband's car to work. *or*
     Elizabeth practically never drives her husband's car to work.

4.   Sandi has only a week to file the tax returns for John.

5.   Scarcely any of the Lakers' players have ever experienced a losing season. *or*
     Practically none of the Lakers' players have ever experienced a losing season.

✔ Writing – Usage Strategy #11:
• Make Correct Comparisons (Comparative and Superlative Degree)

Errors in comparative and superlative degree routinely slip by even the best students. Can you identify the mistake in the following question?

> 10.   Despite <u>reports to the contrary</u>, the coach <u>indicated that he would take</u>
>   (A)   (B)
>   <u>the best of</u> the two gymnasts to the international competition <u>next month</u>.
>   (C)   (D)
>   <u>No error</u>
>   (E)

Because there are only two gymnasts, the word *best* in choice (C) should be replaced with the comparative degree form *better*.

Certain SAT Usage questions may require you to identify incorrectly formed comparisons. **Comparative** refers to the second degree of comparison; the comparative form is used when exactly two items are compared. **Superlative** refers to the third degree of comparison; it is used when three or more items are compared.

Adjectives and Adverbs: Regular Comparison Forms

Description of Adjective or Adverb	How to Form Comparative and Superlative Degrees	Example: Adjective or Adverb	Comparative Degree	Superlative Degree
One syllable word ending in a single consonant	Add -er or -est	tall fast	taller faster	tallest fastest
One syllable word ending in -e	Add -r or -st	fine	finer	finest
Two syllable word ending in -y	Replace the y with i and add -er or -est	pretty	prettier	prettiest
Contains two syllables and does not end in -y **or** Contains three or more syllables	Place the word more or most in front of the adjective or adverb	intelligent	more intelligent	most intelligent

Adjectives and Adverbs: Irregular Comparison Forms

Adjective, Adverb	Comparative	Superlative
bad, badly	worse	worst
good, well	better	best
old (adjective)	older or elder	oldest or eldest
*far	farther or further	farthest or furthest
*little	littler, less or lesser	littlest or least
*much	more	most

* Can be used as an adjective or an adverb.

RULES FOR COMPARATIVE AND SUPERLATIVE DEGREE

1.   **Do not use the superlative degree in place of the comparative degree or vice versa.**

INCORRECT: Of the two horse trainers, Ed is the smartest.

(Because the comparison involves two items, the comparative degree is required.)

CORRECT: Of the two horse trainers, Ed is the smarter.

2.   **Do not incorrectly use *more* or *most* in place of *-er* or *-est* endings.**

INCORRECT: Honey was more fond of playing poker than Aida was.

(The *-er* ending should be used instead of the word *more*.)

CORRECT: Honey was fonder of playing poker than Aida was.

3.   **Do not form a comparison using *more* or *most* in addition to the *-er* or *-est* suffix.**

INCORRECT: During World War II, the Queen Mother was England's most strongest inspirational figure.

(Use the *-est* ending only and drop the word *most*.)

CORRECT: During World War II, the Queen Mother was England's strongest inspirational figure.

4.   **Adjectives that express extreme or absolute conditions cannot be used in the comparative or superlative form.** Words such as *perfect, matchless*, and *unique* are such adjectives. For example, something cannot be *more unique* or *most unique*. There are not various levels of uniqueness. Something is either considered unique or it is not.

✔ Writing – Usage Strategy #12:
• Use Correct Prepositions

Prepositions connect certain words or phrases in a sentence. Pay extra attention to Usage questions in which a preposition immediately following a verb is underlined.

Example:

11.   Sandy and Kirk, <u>who</u> both believe <u>in</u> the therapeutic <u>value of acupuncture,</u>
                          (A)   (B)   (C)
        will participate <u>with</u> the holistic healing seminar. <u>No error</u>
                          (D)   (E)

In the sentence above, the verb/preposition expression *believe in* is correct, but listen to how *participate with* sounds. The preposition *with* is used incorrectly and should be replaced with the word *in*. The answer is (D).

Make sure that verb/preposition phrases are properly stated. Watch for incorrect uses of the following red flag prepositions:

about, against, at, by, for, from, in, of, on, over, to, upon, with

If you ever see any one of the above prepositions in a Usage question, listen to how it sounds in the sentence and ask yourself whether or not a different preposition would sound better.

Example:

INCORRECT: He was accused with committing the crime.

The preposition *with* is used incorrectly again. The correct verb-preposition form is *accused of*, not *accused with*:

CORRECT: He was accused of committing the crime.

✓ **Writing – Usage Strategy #13:**

•   **Eliminate Redundancy**

Rose is a rose is a rose is a rose.

– Gertrude Stein

Watch for Usage questions that contain redundant wording:

12.   Although <u>he did not win</u> much prize money, the game show
            (A)
    <u>contestant received</u> <u>several free gifts</u> from the <u>show's sponsors</u>. <u>No error</u>
            (B)   (C)   (D)   (E)

The phrase *free gifts* in choice (C) presents a redundancy, as any gift is, by definition, free of charge. The word *free* should be eliminated.

Redundancy refers to the unnecessary repetition or restatement of ideas that are implied. The following are classic redundancies. The word or words that should be eliminated are italicized:

> *advance* planning
> *basic* fundamentals
> consensus *of opinion*
> each *and every*
> filled *to capacity*
> *grouped* together
> *pair of* twins
> *serious* crisis
> surrounded *on all sides*
> *unexpected* surprise

You get the idea. Do not say anything twice that you can say once. Whenever an underlined pair of words or short phrase in a Usage question contains redundant wording, it is almost always the error in the sentence.

✓ **Writing – Usage Strategy #14:**

• **Identify Word Choice and Diction Errors**

The following are commonly confused words or short phrases. It is likely that you will encounter a few Usage questions that require you to distinguish between or among them.

Accept/Except

Accept: To receive or to approve
Except: To exclude or to leave out

Affect/Effect

Affect: To influence (verb). *The professional golfers were favorably affected by a welcome break in the hot weather.*
Effect: A result (noun). *The rainfall had a positive effect on Juanita and Melissa's garden.*
    To bring about (verb). *The new policy is intended to effect true change.*

All ways/Always

All ways: Every way. *Dr. O'Connor used all ways available to treat her patients.*
Always: All of the time. *Our cat King always slept on the end of the bed.*

Although/Though

Although: *Although* usually occurs at the beginning of a sentence. *Although Louis could not be found in the genealogical records, we know that he was probably born in Germany.*
Though: *Though* may occur elsewhere and is best used to link words or phrases. *Pepper is a sedate though nimble gal.*

Among/Between

Among: Relates more than two items. *Kim, Holly and Terri talked among themselves.*
Between: Relates two items only. *Ruth usually sat between the two older boys.*

As/Like

As: Conjunction that is followed by a verb. *Patti was as good at gardening as anyone I have ever met.*
Like: Preposition that is not followed by a verb. *Marjan looks like her father.*

Bad/Badly

Bad: (adjective). *Sydney felt bad when she learned that Vaughn had married Lauren.* (The word *felt* is a passive verb that cannot be modified by an adverb; it refers to a state of being that must be modified by an adjective.)
Badly: (adverb). *Arvin acted badly toward Jack.*

Beside/Besides

Beside: Next to
Besides: In addition

Cite/Sight/Site

Cite: To quote. *Sark wasn't sure if the references to Rambaldi were cited correctly.*
Sight: Vision. *His sight improved after he had laser surgery.*
Site: Location. *Uncle Graham took all of us to the site where the pioneers arrived in Emigration Canyon.*

Compare to/Compare with
Compare to: Use when showing how two different things are alike
Compare with: Use when studying two similar things to find similarities/differences

Fewer/Less
Fewer: Use with items that can be counted individually
Less: Use with amounts that are measured by mass

Good/Well
Good: Pleasing (adjective). *The cheesecake tastes good.*
Well: Sufficiently (adverb). *Joan Didion writes exceptionally well.*

Irregardless
An outdated word that is not accepted as formal English; use *regardless* instead.

It's/Its
It's: Contraction of *it is* or *it has*
Its: Possessive pronoun meaning *belonging to it*

Lay/Lie
Lay: (Transitive verb that always takes an object). *Tami lay the reports down on her desk.*
Lie: (Intransitive verb that never takes an object). *Our Basset Hound lies down near our mother's chair.*

Raise/Rise
Raise: To bring up, to lift (transitive verb that takes an object). *We raise the flag in the morning.*
Rise: To get up, to increase (intransitive verb that never takes an object). *They rise for the Pledge of Allegiance.*

Real/Really
Real: Authentic (adjective). *The table is made of real wood.*
Really: Intensely or very (adverb). *Jane Fonda is a really passionate actress.*

Reason is because/Reason is that
Reason is that is the best phrase to use in formal writing. Try to avoid the redundant phrases *the reason is because* or *the reason why.*

Set/Sit
Set: To place an object in a particular position (transitive verb that takes an object). *Lily set the table with new placemats.*
Sit: To rest or be seated (intransitive verb that never takes an object). *We usually sit in the upper deck at Dodger Stadium.*

That/Which/Who
That: Refers to people or things
Which: Always refers to things
Who: Refers to people

Their/There/They're
Their: Belongs to them. *Maggie and Oliver liked to eat their lunch at the same time.*
There: Location. *Dr. Tran's stethoscope is over there.*
They're: Contraction of "they are." *They're going to visit Prince Sebastian.*

Try to/Try and
Use *try to*. A phrase such as *try and listen* implies two different actions when only one is intended.

Weather/Whether
Weather: Climate. *The weather in Southern California is sunny and warm.*
Whether: Refers to a choice. *Whether or not Franklin D. Roosevelt and Winston Churchill were successful in their negotiations at Yalta is the subject of ongoing debate.*

Who/Whom
Who: Used as a subject in a sentence. *Who will be the guest on Oprah Winfrey's show tomorrow?*
Whom: Used as a receiver or indirect object in a sentence. *To whom does this jacket belong?*

Who's/Whose
Who's: Contraction for *who is*
Whose: Possessive pronoun meaning *belongs to whom*

Would of/Would have *(also applies to "should" and "could")*
Would of: Incorrect form of *would have* or *would've*. *I would of fallen* is incorrect and should be *I would have fallen.*
Would have: Should not be used in place of *had* in a conditional statement. *If we had* (not *would have*) *left early, we would have been on time.*

✓ **Writing – Usage Strategy #15:**

•   **Know Correct Punctuation**

A kiss can be a comma, a question mark, or an exclamation point.

– Mistinguett

PUNCTUATION GUIDE

USE A COMMA	CORRECT
Before a coordinating conjunction that joins two independent clauses	We had a chance to tie the game, but our kicker missed a field goal.
After a dependent clause (if found at the beginning of a sentence)	After they left work, Marshall and Weiss got a pizza together.
After an introductory phrase or adverb clause	The writers upstairs have five cats, two of which are twin white Turkish Angoras.
To separate items in a list	Her family members attended Brigham Young University, the University of Utah, Occidental College, and the University of Southern California.
Before and after a parenthetical phrase in a sentence	Eva, our neighbor, was walking her brother's dog.

DO NOT USE A COMMA	INCORRECT	CORRECT
To separate the subject from the predicate	Morris's first car, didn't have air conditioning.	Morris's first car didn't have air conditioning.
To separate a verb from its object, or a preposition from its object	Steve Young passed the ball to Jerry Rice, for the 49ers' winning touchdown.	Steve Young passed the ball to Jerry Rice for the 49ers' winning touchdown.
After a coordinating conjunction	Rene finished her work so, she went home early.	Rene finished her work, so she went home early.
After very short introductory phrases *(In some instances placement of this comma is considered optional and not incorrect.)*	After dinner, Jaci started the meeting. *(The comma in this sentence is not necessary, but it is not used incorrectly.)*	After dinner Jaci started the meeting.
Before and after a restrictive phrase	Those people, at the training seminar, are Richard's friends.	Those people at the training seminar are Richard's friends.
Before the first or after the last items in a list	Leola cooked, gumbo, rice, and pralines, for lunch.	Leola cooked gumbo, rice, and pralines for lunch.

A period is a stop sign. A semicolon is a rolling stop sign;
a comma is merely an amber light.

– Andrew Offutt

USE A SEMI-COLON	CORRECT
In place of a coordinating conjunction to join two closely related independent clauses	The growing company is based in Lincoln, Nebraska; its other offices are in Shanghai and New York.

DO NOT USE A SEMI-COLON	INCORRECT	CORRECT
To join a dependent clause with an independent clause	Because of the rain; David and Samantha's tournament was delayed.	Because of the rain, David and Samantha's tournament was delayed.
Before a coordinating conjunction that joins two independent clauses, unless the clauses already have many commas in them	They were married in Montecito; and they honeymooned in Acapulco.	They were married in Montecito, and they honeymooned in Acapulco.

USE A COLON	CORRECT
After an independent clause to introduce a list or thought	She had only one goal: to write her family history.

DO NOT USE A COLON	INCORRECT	CORRECT
Between a verb and its object or subject complement, or between a preposition and its object	Cliff and Kaenan gave their grandfather: a new tennis racquet and several tennis balls. Manuela heard the news from: Courtney and Elisabeth.	Cliff and Kaenan gave their grandfather a new tennis racquet and several tennis balls. Manuela heard the news from Courtney and Elisabeth.

Quotation Marks:

Apply double quotation marks (") before and after direct quotations in speech or written material. Remember to use quotation marks to identify small pieces of work, such as short stories, poems, songs, articles in newspapers, etc. Use quotation marks with other forms of punctuation correctly:

1. **Periods** and **commas** are contained **within quotation marks.**

    Singing "Stand Back," Stevie Nicks whirled around the stage with her tambourine.

2. **Semicolons** and **colons** are used **outside of quotation marks.**

    The message is clear in the story "The Lottery": humans can be animals.

3. **Question marks, exclamation points,** and **dashes** are **contained within quotation marks when they are in the quotation, but outside when they are not.**

    Will Fleetwood Mac play the song "Rhiannon"?

    "Was the satellite launched into orbit?" Dianne asked Lesley.

Use single quotation marks (') to signify quotations within a quotation.

    "She read 'The Bear' and decided that Faulkner is America's greatest author," the professor explained.

Apostrophe:

1. Use an **apostrophe** to form a **contraction** or the **possessive case** of a noun.

    The novelist doesn't drive her black sports car when it's raining.

    LaVell Edwards Stadium, formerly Cougar Stadium, is Provo's largest arena.

2. Add an **apostrophe** after the *s* at the end of a **plural possessive** noun.

    After the show, Jessica and Patty applauded all of the actors' performances.

Dash:

1. To **emphasize a parenthetical phrase**, use a **dash** instead of comma.

    Alisa bought hotdogs – not hamburgers – for the family picnic.

2. A **dash** may also be used **to end a list** with a conclusion.

    Springfield, Seattle, and Jacksonville – these are good cities in which to raise children.

NOTE: SAT Writing questions do not typically cover end punctuation (use of periods, question marks or exclamation points).

I never made a mistake in grammar but one in my life
and as soon as I done it I seen it.

– Carl Sandburg

PRACTICE EXERCISES
USAGE & GRAMMAR (IDENTIFYING SENTENCE ERRORS)

1. Monkeys <u>climbing</u> high in the trees <u>while eating</u> wild berries <u>underneath</u> the branches, unaware of the zebras
        (A)   (B)   (C)
    <u>nipping</u> at their tails. <u>No error</u>
      (D)   (E)

2. <u>Although</u> the <u>school's new nurse</u> did not believe the student was ill, she <u>is allowing</u> him <u>to miss</u> fifth period.
      (A)   (B)   (C)   (D)
    <u>No error</u>
      (E)

3. It is <u>neither</u> unexpected <u>nor</u> inconvenient that <u>either</u> Joy or Shelley will probably <u>join up with</u> us later at the
            (A)   (B)   (C)   (D)
    concert. <u>No error</u>
                (E)

4. Terry and <u>him</u> are planning to go to Hawaii <u>right after</u> they <u>strike it rich</u> panning for gold in <u>parts unknown</u>.
              (A)   (B)   (C)   (D)
    <u>No error</u>
      (E)

5. Of the two finalists, the younger girl was the <u>most competitive</u> in <u>each event</u>; she <u>could not stand</u> to lose to
                                                      (A)   (B)   (C)
    anyone <u>under any circumstances</u>. <u>No error</u>
              (D)   (E)

6. <u>Should</u> you go to the mountains <u>along</u> the state's northern border, every rest stop <u>offers</u> <u>one</u> a tremendous
      (A)   (B)   (C)   (D)
    panoramic view of the valley below. <u>No error</u>
                                            (E)

7. If I <u>would have</u> concentrated on the exam I <u>might have been</u> able to get an A <u>in the course</u>, <u>demanding</u> as it
          (A)   (B)   (C)   (D)
    was. <u>No error</u>
            (E)

8. We <u>do not doubt</u> that the county officials intend to divide the land <u>between</u> the three farmers, but the
          (A)   (B)
    <u>fact of the matter</u> is that they <u>have not been</u> able to do so. <u>No error</u>
        (C)   (D)   (E)

9. When we <u>all</u> go on our <u>upcoming</u> Caribbean cruise <u>we are going</u> to go snorkeling, fishing, swimming, and
            (A)   (B)   (C)
    <u>sleep</u> in the sun. <u>No error</u>
      (D)   (E)

10. The movie was <u>far scarier</u> than I expected it to be, but I <u>can't</u> hardly believe how <u>limited</u> the special <u>effects</u>
                (A)   (B)   (C)   (D)
    were. <u>No error</u>
          (E)

11. Kerry used <u>to attend</u> a class <u>where</u> the instructor, instead <u>of assigning</u> written homework, required students
               (A)   (B)   (C)
    <u>to visit</u> various museums. <u>No error</u>
     (D)   (E)

12. It <u>used to be</u> that <u>Lincoln's and Washington's</u> birthdays <u>were celebrated separately</u>, but now they are both
       (A)   (B)   (C)
    commemorated in <u>mid-February</u> on President's Day. <u>No error</u>
              (D)   (E)

13. A difficult employee is one <u>who</u> takes too much time for lunch, makes <u>a lot</u> of personal phone calls, is usually
                    (A)   (B)
    late for work, and doesn't <u>ever</u> finish <u>their</u> daily tasks. <u>No error</u>
           (C)   (D)   (E)

14. We <u>were planning</u> a trip to <u>New Zealand, however,</u> when we phoned the airlines, we <u>found out</u> that there were
       (A)   (B)   (C)
    <u>no</u> flights available. <u>No error</u>
   (D)   (E)

15. <u>When watching soccer</u> <u>on television</u>, the players' sudden movements are <u>often hard</u> <u>to follow</u>. <u>No error</u>
        (A)   (B)   (C)   (D)   (E)

16. The artist <u>beautifully portraying</u> the Medici family <u>by combining</u> oil paints and textured fabrics <u>to create</u> a
            (A)   (B)   (C)
    <u>unique</u> mural. <u>No error</u>
   (D)   (E)

17. Jan and Fran, <u>having waited</u> in line <u>for a long time</u> at the home improvement store, <u>fully expressed</u> their
               (A)   (B)   (C)
    considerable annoyance <u>at my dinner party</u>. <u>No error</u>
                (D)   (E)

18. Catherine and Tracey were <u>on their way</u> to the jewelry mart when they <u>stop</u> to fill the car <u>with</u> unleaded
                    (A)   (B)   (C)
    gasoline at the <u>furthest</u> pump from the cashier. <u>No error</u>
          (D)   (E)

19. Adan thinks that the small diner <u>on San Francisco's Nob Hill</u> is <u>as good</u> <u>as any</u> restaurant <u>in all of</u> the city.
                        (A)   (B)   (C)   (D)
    <u>No error</u>
      (E)

20. After she returns from New Orleans, Jill <u>will have to decide</u> fairly quickly <u>whether or not</u> she wants
                                                  (A)   (B)

    <u>to accept placement</u> at the nursing school's new <u>site.</u> <u>No error</u>
            (C)   (D)   (E)

Answer Explanations:

1.   (A)   Sentence fragment. The sentence lacks a main verb. *Climbing* should be used with a helping verb, e.g. *were climbing*.

2.   (C)   Verb tense error. The verb phrase *did not believe* is a past tense construction; *is allowing* should be replaced with *allowed*.

3.   (D)   Idiom error. *Join up with* should be replaced with *join*.

4.   (A)   Pronoun case error. Use *he* instead of *him*.

5.   (A)   Error in comparative degree. Use *more* not *most* when comparing two people or things.

6.   (D)   Change in pronoun person from second person to third person. Use *you* instead of *one*.

7.   (A)   Error in verb tense. When a clause begins with *if*, use *had* (past perfect) in place of *would have*.

8.   (B)   Word choice error. Use the word *among* instead of *between* to relate more than two items.

9.   (D)   Faulty parallelism. *Sleep* is not parallel with the other *-ing* endings in *snorkeling*, *fishing* and *swimming*.

10. (B)   Double negative. *Can't* and *hardly* are both negative words. Change *can't* to *can*.

11. (B)   Idiom error. *Where* should be replaced with *in which*.

12. (E)   No error.

13. (D)   Pronoun-antecedent agreement error. The pronoun *their* is plural and does not agree with the singular antecedent *one*. Substitute *his* for *their*.

14. (B)   Comma splice. *However* should not be used as a conjunction joining two independent clauses. A semi-colon or period should be used to separate the clauses.

15. (A)   Dangling participle. The phrase *when watching soccer* does not modify any noun or pronoun.

16. (A)   Sentence fragment. There is no main verb; *-ing* forms of the verb require helping verbs. Use *portrayed* instead of *portraying*.

17. (D)   Misplaced modifier. *At my dinner party* is incorrectly placed to modify *annoyance*; it sounds as if the annoyance is a result of the dinner party. The sentence should read: *At my dinner party, Jan and Fran fully expressed their considerable annoyance about having waited in line for a long time at the home improvement store.*

18. (B)   Verb tense error. The sentence begins in the past tense. Change *stop* to *stopped*.

19. (C)   Faulty comparison. The word *other* should be included when comparing something to its broader group. *As any* should be replaced with *as any other*.

20. (E)   No error.

Writing
Chapter 2

Improving Sentences

Strategies:

1. Directions for Improving Sentences & How the Questions Will Look

2. Avoid Wordy Answer Choices

3. Active vs. Passive Voice

4. Sentence Fragments

5. Run-on Sentences

6. Faulty Parallelism

7. Faulty Comparison

8. Errors in Coordination and Subordination

9. Mixed Constructions

✓ **Writing – Improving Sentences Strategy #1:**

• **Know How the Questions Will Look**

The second question type on the SAT Writing section is called Improving Sentences. A sentence is provided, an underlined portion of which may be stated in a better way. Following the sentence are answer choices (A) – (E). Choice (A) repeats the original underlined portion, meaning that no correction is needed. Choices (B) – (E) represent alternative phrasings.

Example:

1. The school board wants to begin year-end skills testing in every grade level <u>and also strengthening core curriculum subjects.</u>

   (A) and also strengthening core curriculum subjects.
   (B) and to strengthen core curriculum subjects.
   (C) and makes stronger core curriculum subjects.
   (D) and the core curriculum subjects are also strengthened.
   (E) and also will strengthen the core curriculum subjects.

The answer to this question is (B). There is an error in the original sentence that relates to parallel structure. The second verb phrase used must match the form of the first; *to begin* and *strengthening* are not in parallel form. *Strengthening* should be replaced by *to strengthen*.

This chapter outlines concepts that are addressed by the SAT's Improving Sentences items. The previous chapter covering usage and grammar should also be studied with respect to this question type.

✓ **Writing – Improving Sentences Strategy #2:**

• **Avoid Wordy Answer Choices**

For Improving Sentences items, the best answer choice:

• **Is clear and concise**
• **Effectively and precisely restates the underlined portion of the sentence**
• **Is free of redundancy and awkward phrasing**

Here is the single best tip for answering these questions:

WORDY ANSWER CHOICES ARE USUALLY WRONG.

As is the case with Usage questions, corrected Improving Sentences items also sound right. Make sure that your corrected version does not sound strange or awkward.

✓ **Writing – Improving Sentences Strategy #3:**

• **Choose the Active Voice**

Transitive verbs must be accompanied by direct objects to complete their meaning. *Example:*

> Dan approved the manuscript.

In the sentence above, *Dan* is the subject, *approved* is the verb, and *manuscript* is the direct object. This sentence has an active voice construction. If the subject and direct object switch places, the subject becomes the recipient of the action. The sentence above is rearranged in this way:

> The manuscript was approved by Dan.

This new version uses the passive voice.

Active voice: The subject performs an action.

Passive voice: The subject is the recipient of the action. The verb includes a form of "to be" plus the past participle of another verb.

Active voice sentences are more direct and dynamic than passive voice constructions. *Here is another example:*

Passive voice: World history is studied by high school sophomores.

To transform this sentence into the active voice, move *high school sophomores* to the beginning of the sentence and *world history* to the end of the sentence; then change the verb to the present tense.

Active voice (preferred):   High school sophomores study world history.

Try the following Improving Sentences item:

2.   During the late spring storm, <u>the newly planted flowers were covered by a light snowfall.</u>

   (A)   the newly planted flowers were covered by a light snowfall.
   (B)   the newly planted flowers covered by a light snowfall.
   (C)   a light snowfall was covering the newly planted flowers.
   (D)   a light snowfall covered the newly planted flowers.
   (E)   a light snowfall had been covering the newly planted flowers.

The underlined portion of this sentence shifts to the passive voice. Choice (B) is incorrect because it turns the sentence into a sentence fragment. Choices (C) and (E) are active constructions but they use incorrect verb tenses. Choice (D) is correct, as it presents an active construction with the correct past tense form of the verb.

✓ Writing – Improving Sentences Strategy #4:
•   Identify Sentence Fragments

A sentence fragment is an incomplete sentence. It usually lacks a subject or a verb. *Example:*

INCOMPLETE: The twin Siamese kittens peering out of their cage at the pet store.

This statement does not sound like a complete thought because it lacks a true verb. The following corrected versions add a needed verb:

COMPLETE: The twin Siamese kittens *are* peering out of their cage at the pet store.

or

COMPLETE: The twin Siamese kittens peering out of their cage at the pet store *will* soon *come* home with us.

The following is a sample Improving Sentences question involving a sentence fragment. Attempt to solve the question by "hearing" the error.

3.   <u>The culturally advanced Indian civilization existing</u> to the north of the Platte River.

    (A)   The culturally advanced Indian civilization existing
    (B)   The Indian civilization with its cultural advancement having existed
    (C)   The culturally advanced Indian civilization have existed
    (D)   The culturally advanced Indian civilization exists
    (E)   The existing of the culturally advanced Indian civilization

The problem centers again around the lack of a correctly used verb. The word *existing* sounds like a verb, but it is not. Answer choices (B) and (E) also present sentence fragments. Choice (C) contains an error in subject – verb agreement; *civilization* is singular while *have existed* is plural. The answer is (D) because it replaces the word *existing* with *exists*.

✓ Writing – Improving Sentences Strategy #5:
•   Recognize Run-on Sentences

A run-on sentence consists of two sentences, or independent clauses, incorrectly joined as one sentence. If two independent clauses are connected by only a comma, the error is known as a comma splice. *Example:*

    Jennifer interviewed several applicants, she hired those who had strong letters of recommendation.

A run-on sentence can be fixed in one of three ways:

Punctuation	Example
Use a period and make two sentences.	Jennifer interviewed several <u>applicants. She</u> hired those who had strong letters of recommendation. *(Please note that using a period to make two sentences is not an option presented in the Improving Sentences section of the SAT, but it may be an option in the Improving Paragraphs section.)*
Use a semi-colon.	Jennifer interviewed several <u>applicants; she</u> hired those who had strong letters of recommendation.
Use a comma with a conjunction.	Jennifer interviewed several <u>applicants, and</u> she hired those who had strong letters of recommendation.

Use the information presented in the table above to identify the correct answer for the following Improving Sentences item:

4.   <u>The matinee will end early,</u> we can go to the party afterwards.

   (A)   The matinee will end early,
   (B)   The matinee will end early; and
   (C)   The matinee will end early, so
   (D)   The matinee being over early,
   (E)   Because the matinee will end early so

The question presents a run-on sentence with a comma splice. Choice (B) is incorrect because a semi-colon is not used with a conjunction. Choice (D) is an awkward construction. Choice (E) incorrectly uses two conjunctions instead of one (*because* and *so*). Choice (C) is correct because it adds a conjunction after the comma.

✓ Writing – Improving Sentences Strategy #6:
•   Be Aware of Faulty Parallelism

When a series of items is listed in a sentence, they should be presented in what is known as "parallel structure." The following is an example of faulty parallelism:

INCORRECT: When Erin and her family go on vacation, they like to swim, to relax on the beach, and going shopping.

To swim and *to relax* follow the same "to _____" format, but *going shopping* does not.

CORRECT: When Erin and her family go on vacation, they like to swim, to relax on the beach, and to shop.

Try the following Improving Sentences item concerning parallel structure:

5.   The president plans to provide a plan to financially assist the impoverished <u>as well as reducing income tax for the middle class.</u>

   (A)   as well as reducing income tax for the middle class.
   (B)   as well as to reduce income tax for the middle class.
   (C)   as well as giving the middle class a tax break.
   (D)   and the middle class are also provided with a tax break.
   (E)   and to give a reduced tax rate to the middle class additionally.

The underlined portion of the sentence is not parallel with its beginning; *to provide* and *reducing* are not in parallel form. Choice (C) is incorrect because *to provide* and *giving* are also not in parallel form. Choice (D) is incorrect because the sentence does not follow parallel form and it shifts from the active to the passive voice. Choice (E) is incorrect because the word *additionally* is located too far from the verb *give* that it modifies. Choice (B) is the right answer; *to provide* and *to reduce* are in parallel form.

| ✓   **Writing – Improving Sentences Strategy #7:** |
| **•   Find Faulty Comparisons** |

Comparison errors are similar in nature to faulty parallelism. **When two things are compared in a sentence, the items must be presented in the same grammatical form using the same parts of speech.** The following sentence illustrates a comparison error:

INCORRECT: Emma thinks that singing in the school choir is more enjoyable than theatre performance.

In this sentence, *singing in the school choir* is a gerund phrase and *theatre performance* is a noun phrase, so the comparison made is illogical. To fix the sentence, the items compared must be in the same form:

CORRECT: Emma thinks that singing in the school choir is more enjoyable than performing in the theatre.

INCOMPLETE COMPARISONS: Incomplete comparisons occur when the compared item is implied but not stated. *Examples:*

INCOMPLETE: Students who study usually perform better on tests.

INCOMPLETE: The new format of the SAT exam is more challenging.

Correct incomplete comparisons by adding the word "than" and stating the item with which the first item is compared:

COMPLETE: Students who study usually perform better on tests *than students who do not study much.*

COMPLETE: The new format of the SAT exam is more challenging *than the former version.*

ILLOGICAL COMPARISIONS: Illogical comparisons result when two items are unlike in nature or when the second item only partially relates to the first. *Examples:*

INCORRECT: My flight to Salt Lake City was much shorter than my brother.

INCORRECT: The historical sites and museums we visited in Canada were similar to anywhere in the United States.

The first sentence illogically compares *my flight* with *my brother* and the second illogically compares the *historical sites and museums I visited in Canada* with *anywhere in the United States.* Revise the sentences so that the items compared are of like kind by repeating key words and by using the same grammatical form for items compared:

CORRECT: *My flight* to Salt Lake City was much longer than *my brother's flight* was.

CORRECT: The *historical sites and museums we visited in Canada* were similar to *historical sites and museums anywhere in the United States.*

The following Improving Sentences item contains a comparison error:

6.   My mother believes that <u>water skiing is more dangerous than a motorcycle</u>.

(A)   water skiing is more dangerous than a motorcycle.
(B)   water skiing is more dangerous than to ride a motorcycle.
(C)   water skiing is more dangerous than riding a motorcycle.
(D)   to water ski is more dangerous than a motorcycle.
(E)   the danger of water skiing is worse than motorcycles.

In this sentence, *water skiing* is illogically compared to *motorcycle.* Answer choice (B) is not in parallel form. Answer choices (D) and (E) also present faulty comparisons; in (D), *to water ski* is a different part of speech (verb) than *motorcycle* (noun), and in (E), *the danger of water skiing* is illogically compared to *motorcycles.* Choice (C) is correct because *water skiing* is the same grammatical form as *riding a motorcycle.*

> ✓ **Writing – Improving Sentences Strategy #8:**
>
> •   **Identify Errors in Coordination or Subordination**

FAULTY COORDINATION

Coordinating conjunctions (*and, but, nor, or, for, so* and *yet*) are meant to connect two independent clauses containing ideas equivalent in significance. **Faulty coordination provides equal emphasis to disproportionate or unrelated clauses.** *Example:*

INCORRECT: Shakespeare wrote many great sonnets and plays and he lived in London in the 16th century.

The idea that *Shakespeare wrote many great sonnets* is of far greater significance than the fact that *he lived in London in the 16th century.*

To fix this error, use a subordinating conjunction or relative pronoun *(see below)* and state the less important idea within an embedded dependent clause:

CORRECT: Shakespeare, who lived in London in the 16th century, wrote many great sonnets and plays.

Coordination errors can also occur when the incorrect coordinating conjunction is selected. *Example:*

INCORRECT: Clara Lou wanted to support her candidate, *but* she went to the political rally.

The conjunction does not correctly coordinate, or match, the idea in the first independent clause with the idea in the second independent clause. The sentence should read as follows:

CORRECT: Clara Lou wanted to support her candidate, *so* she went to the political rally.

FAULTY SUBORDINATION

As shown above, **subordination** is a method of presenting ideas of unequal importance. **Subordinate clauses** are dependent noun, adjective or adverb clauses that are introduced by subordinating conjunctions (including *after, although, as, as if, because, before, even though, if, in order that, once, since, so, than, though, unless, until, when, where, whether, while*) or relative pronouns (*that, which, who, whom, whose*).

Faulty subordination results when the expected relation between the main clause and the subordinate clause is reversed or when the more important clause is placed in the subordinate position. *Example:*

INCORRECT: Styrofoam products are very popular for picnics although they are not biodegradable and they present an ongoing environmental challenge with respect to land pollution.

In a composition about land pollution, this sentence would take attention away from the principle subject and incorrectly emphasize the popularity of Styrofoam products. The faulty subordination can be corrected by changing the position of the subordinating word or phrase.

CORRECT: Although Styrofoam products are very popular for picnics, they are not biodegradable and they present an ongoing environmental challenge with respect to land pollution.

Faulty subordination can also occur when the content of the dependent and independent clauses is not logically related. *Example:*

INCORRECT: Because it is still widely discussed among both politicians and military leaders, the Vietnam War remains controversial.

This construction makes it sound as if the discussions about the war are the source of the controversy.

CORRECT: Because the Vietnam War remains controversial, it is still widely discussed among both politicians and military leaders.

A third type of subordination error occurs when a supposed sentence contains two or more subordinate or dependent clauses but no main clause, resulting in a sentence fragment. *Example:*

INCORRECT: Driving to school in the early morning and then opening my locker.

This word group is not a sentence at all; it is a sentence fragment containing two subordinate clauses – *driving to school in the early morning* and *opening my locker*. There is no stated subject or verb. The following version is a complete sentence that corrects this problem:

CORRECT: I drove to school in the early morning and then opened my locker.

A fourth type of subordination error occurs when the incorrect subordinating conjunction is selected. *Example:*

INCORRECT: *Despite* her extensive course work in human anatomy, Jenny is a strong candidate for medical school.

The subordinating conjunction *despite* does not match the content of the sentence.

CORRECT: *Due to* her extensive course work in human anatomy, Jenny is a strong candidate for medical school.

The Improving Sentences item that follows contains both a coordination and a subordination error:

7.   <u>Crystal and Delisa ended up going to the movies although they wanted to go to the beach, but</u> they didn't need suntan lotion after all.

(A)   Crystal and Delisa ended up going to the movies although they wanted to go to the beach, but

(B)   Crystal and Delisa ended up going to the movies even though they wanted to go to the beach, so

(C)   Crystal and Delisa ended up going to the movies instead of the beach where they wanted to go, so

(D)   Although Crystal and Delisa wanted to go to the beach, they ended up going to the movies, but

(E)   Although Crystal and Delisa wanted to go to the beach, they ended up going to the movies, so

The first part of the original sentence (up to the comma) is awkward because its main clause and subordinate clause are incorrectly sequenced. The second part of the sentence is an independent clause introduced by the incorrect coordinating conjunction *but*. Choice (B) repeats the subordination error, choice (C) is a wordy and awkward construction, and choice (D) repeats the coordination error. Choice (E) is correct because the main and subordinate clauses are in the correct sequence in the first part of the sentence, and the coordinating conjunction *so* correctly begins the second independent clause.

✓ Writing – Improving Sentences Strategy #9:
- **Spot Mixed Constructions**

A *mixed construction* occurs when a sentence starts with one grammatical form and then derails with another. These are groups of words that do not quite measure up to being true sentences; they sound as if the writer lost track of what he was saying and where he was headed.

A classic mixed construction starts with a subordinate clause, prepositional phrase or other modifier that is not followed by an independent clause containing a stated subject. It is a subject-less attempt at a sentence. *Example:*

INCORRECT: Although she comes from a foreign country, does not prevent her from running for political office.

The opening dependent clause appropriately begins the sentence, but it should be followed by an independent clause; instead, there is a phrase including a verb but no subject. To correct the mixed construction, add a true subject:

CORRECT: Although she comes from a foreign country, *her immigrant status* does not prevent her from running for political office.

Take a look at this Improving Sentences item:

8.   For many who experience chronic dehydration, <u>increases the probability of forming kidney stones.</u>

(A)   increases the probability of forming kidney stones.
(B)   can increase the probability of forming kidney stones.
(C)   the probability of forming kidney stones increases.
(D)   the kidney stone probability increases.
(E)   there is an increased probability in the forming of kidney stones.

This mixed construction begins with a modifier for which there is no subject. Choice (B) also fails to include a subject. Choice (D)'s phrase *kidney stone probability* is non-standard, and choice (E) is wordy and clumsy. Choice (C) correctly fixes the sentence by turning the word *probability* into the subject.

PRACTICE EXERCISES
IMPROVING SENTENCES

1. It has gotten to the point <u>where</u> his relatives on the East Coast rarely visit.

   (A) where
   (B) that
   (C) in which
   (D) to which
   (E) so

2. In 1986 the Statue of Liberty <u>turned 100 years old, she is our most important national landmark</u>.

   (A) turned 100 years old, she is our most important national landmark.
   (B) turned 100 years old; she is our most important national landmark.
   (C) turned 100 years old which is our most important national landmark.
   (D) turning 100 years old, is our most important national landmark.
   (E) had turned 100 years old and so she is our most important national landmark.

3. <u>When officials finally included the sport of curling in the Winter Olympics, the public thought it</u> was boring and hard to understand.

   (A) When officials finally included the sport of curling in the Winter Olympics, the public thought it
   (B) When it was finally included in the Olympics, they found curling
   (C) The Olympics got the sport of curling finally and the public thought it
   (D) The public, when curling finally got introduced in the Olympics, thought it
   (E) Finally the Olympics had curling introduced and the public thought it

4. I cannot look up to anyone who robs banks for a living, <u>despite whatever good they might do with the money</u>.

   (A) despite whatever good might they do with the money.
   (B) although you might think he does good things with the money.
   (C) despite whatever good he might do with the money.
   (D) robbers could do good things with the money, though.
   (E) one cannot justify it by spending the money well.

5. <u>The reason why he gave the test out early was because</u> he wanted us to have enough time to finish it.

   (A) The reason why he gave the test out early was because
   (B) He gave the test out early because
   (C) Because the test was given out early;
   (D) The test, which was given out early because
   (E) He gave the test out early, the reason why being that

6. Across the street from the library, on either side of the gymnasium, <u>was a restaurant and a grocery store</u>.

   (A) was a restaurant and a grocery store.
   (B) existing a restaurant and a grocery store.
   (C) were a restaurant and a grocery store.
   (D) a restaurant and a grocery store exists.
   (E) were a restaurant, a grocery store.

7. <u>Everyone except him and me think</u> we should go home before the second act of the play began.

   (A) Everyone except him and me think
   (B) Everyone except he and I thinks
   (C) Everyone except he and me thinks
   (D) Everyone except him and I thinks
   (E) Everyone except him and me thinks

8. <u>If one is going to attend an outdoor sporting event, you should</u> take a blanket and an umbrella in case it starts to rain.

(A) If one is going to attend an outdoor sporting event, you should

(B) During one's attendance an outdoor sporting event, you might

(C) If you are going to attend an outdoor sporting event, you should

(D) When you go to an outdoor sports event, one should

(E) If you are planning to attend an outdoor sports event, one may

9. <u>When swimming the English Channel,</u> the best route from the shores of England to the cliffs of France is not well defined.

(A) When swimming the English channel,

(B) While swimming inside the English channel,

(C) Swimmers crossing the English channel find that

(D) In swimming the English channel,

(E) Because swimmers cross the English channel,

10. <u>If she finished all of her shopping first,</u> she should have waited in the car for the rest of us.

(A) If she finished all of her shopping first,

(B) If she would have finished all of her shopping first,

(C) If her shopping was finished first,

(D) If she had finished her shopping first,

(E) Her shopping, having been finished first,

11. <u>Visitors are welcome to come to the archaeology site except in December where ancient fossils can be viewed every other month.</u>

(A) Visitors are welcome to come to the archaeology site except in December where ancient fossils can be viewed every other month.

(B) During every month except December, visitors are welcome to come to the archaeology site where they can view ancient fossils.

(C) The archaeology site where, every month except December, ancient fossils can be viewed, is open for visitors.

(D) Visiting in every month except December, ancient fossils can be viewed at a welcoming archaeology site.

(E) Visitors are welcome to visit the archaeology site every month except December where ancient fossils can be viewed.

12. <u>Inquiries and curiosity about the county fair has arisen</u> since the goats arrived.

(A) Inquiries and curiosity about the county fair has arisen

(B) There has been an increase in curiosity and inquiries about the county fair

(C) The county fair, having inquiries and curiosity

(D) From many inquiries and curiosity to boot, the county fair has risen

(E) Curiosity and inquiries about the county fair increasing

13. <u>After taking the train for four hours,</u> a limousine took us the rest of the way.

(A) After taking the train for four hours,

(B) Having been upon the train for four hours,

(C) We rode the train for four hours, and

(D) For four hours we rode the train,

(E) The train was ridden for four hours by us, and

14. Despite the concrete facts about the needed legis-
    lation, everybody is developing <u>their own opinion
    about what Congress should do</u>.

(A) their own opinion about what Congress should do.

(B) their own opinions about what Congress should do.

(C) our own opinions about what Congress should do.

(D) his own individual opinion about what Congress
    should do.

(E) his own opinion about what Congress should do.

15. <u>There are numerous of Julia Child's recipes that
    almost anyone can understand how to prepare in
    her newest cookbook.</u>

(A) There are numerous of Julia Child's recipes that
    almost anyone can understand how to prepare in
    her newest cookbook.

(B) Anyone can prepare recipes from Julia Child's
    newest cookbook, numerous of them are easy to
    understand.

(C) In her newest cookbook, Julia Child offers
    numerous recipes that almost anyone can prepare.

(D) Numerous of Julia Child's recipes, offered in her
    new cookbook, are easily understood by almost
    anyone.

(E) Preparing recipes from her cookbook, Julia Child
    offers anyone numerous recipes that are easy to
    understand.

ANSWER EXPLANATIONS
IMPROVING SENTENCES

1. (B)
(A) Idiom error.
(C) Idiom error.
(D) Idiom error.
(E) Awkward construction.

2. (B)
(A) Comma splice. Independent clauses cannot be joined with a comma.
(C) Clumsy construction and run-on sentence.
(D) Verb tense error and comma splice. The sentence refers to a past event. *Turning* refers to an event in progress. The conjunction *and* should also appear before the word *is.*
(E) Verb tense error. The sentence refers to a past event. The past tense *turned* should be used instead of *had turned.* The meaning of the sentence is also changed by the phrase *and so she is,* which implies that the Statue of Liberty was not our most important national landmark until she turned 100. This is also a clumsy construction.

3. (A)
(B) Ambiguous pronoun reference. There is no specific referent for the pronoun *they.*
(C) Clumsy construction. The adverb *finally* is placed too far away from the verb *got.*
(D) Faulty subordination. *When curling finally got introduced in the Olympics* should precede *the public.*
(E) Shift from passive to active voice. *Had curling introduced* is the passive voice and the *public thought* is the active voice.

4. (C)
(A) Pronoun-antecedent agreement error. *Anyone* is singular; *they* is plural.
(B) Shift in pronoun person. The sentence shifts from the first person, *I,* to second person, *you.*
(D) Comma splice. Two independent clauses cannot be joined with a comma.
(E) Shift in pronoun person and comma splice. The sentence shifts from the first person, *I,* to third

person, *one.* Two independent clauses cannot be joined with a comma.

5. (B)
(A) Wordiness. *The reason why* is redundant and the phrase *was because* is non-idiomatic.
(C) Punctuation error and subordination error. A semi-colon is used to separate two independent clauses. The construction preceding the semi-colon is a dependent clause. A comma should be used instead.
(D) Sentence fragment and awkward construction. There is no main verb present.
(E) Clumsy construction. The comma should be eliminated and the phrase *the reason why being that* should be replaced with the subordinating conjunction *because.*

6. (C)
(A) Subject-verb agreement error. *Was* is singular; *restaurant and grocery store* is a plural subject.
(B) Sentence fragment.
(D) Subject-verb agreement error. *Exists* is singular; *restaurant and grocery store* is a plural subject.
(E) Punctuation error. The word *and* should be used instead of a comma.

7. (E)
(A) Subject-verb agreement. *Everyone* is singular; *think* is plural.
(B) Pronoun choice. Objective case pronouns are required following a preposition (*except*).
(C) Pronoun choice. Objective case pronouns are required following a preposition (*except*).
(D) Pronoun choice. Objective case pronouns are required following a preposition (*except*).

8. (C)
(A) Shift in pronoun person. The sentence shifts from the third person, *one,* to second person, *you.*
(B) Shift in pronoun person. The sentence shifts from the third person, *one,* to second person, *you.*
(D) Shift in pronoun person. The sentence shifts from the second person, *you,* to third person, *one.*
(E) Shift in pronoun person. The sentence shifts from the second person, *you,* to third person, *one.*

9. (C)
(A) Dangling participle. The noun *route* is not properly modified by *when swimming the English Channel*. It is not the *route* that did the swimming.
(B) Dangling participle. The noun *route* is not properly modified by *while swimming inside the English Channel*. It is not the *route* that did the swimming. The word *inside* is also improperly used (diction error). *Inside the* should either be omitted or replaced with the word *in*.
(D) Dangling participle. The noun *route* is not properly modified by *in swimming the English Channel*. It is not the *route* that did the swimming.
(E) Faulty subordination. The subordinating conjunction *because* does not logically connect the sentences' two clauses.

10. (D)
(A) Verb tense error. This is a conditional sentence in which both verb phrases require the past perfect tense. Replace the past tense *finished* with the past perfect tense *had finished*.
(B) Verb tense error. *Would have finished* should be replaced with *had finished*.
(C) Verb tense error and passive construction. Correct with an active voice clause using the past perfect verb tense *had finished*.
(E) Dangling participle. The pronoun *she* is not correctly modified by *her shopping*. This phrasing is also an awkward passive construction that fails to utilize the correct past perfect verb tense *had finished*.

11. (B)
(A) Awkward construction. The phrases *every other month* and *except December* should not be separated.
(C) Awkward passive voice construction. The subject *archaeology* is positioned too far away from the verb *is*.
(D) Dangling participle. The phrase *visiting in every month except December* does not modify *ancient fossils*.
(E) Misplaced modifier. The clause that starts *where ancient fossils can be viewed* modifies *December* instead of *archaeology site*. This is also a passive voice construction.

12. (B)
(A) Subject-verb agreement, incorrect word choice and passive construction. *Inquiries and curiosity* is a plural subject; *has arisen* is a singular verb. *Arisen* is incorrectly used and should be replaced with *risen*.
(C) Awkward construction and sentence fragment. The *-ing* form of a verb requires a helping verb.
(D) Awkward construction with idiom error (*to boot*). Incorrectly used modifier: it is *interest*, not the *country fair*, that has *risen*.
(E) Sentence fragment. The *-ing* form of a verb requires a helping verb.

13. (C)
(A) Dangling participle. *After taking the train for four hours* does not modify *limousine*.
(B) Dangling participle. *Having been upon the train for four hours* does not modify *limousine*.
(D) Comma splice. A comma cannot separate two independent clauses.
(E) Passive construction.

14. (E)
(A) Pronoun-antecedent agreement. *Everybody* is singular; *their* is plural.
(B) Pronoun-antecedent agreement. *Everybody* is singular; *their* is plural.
(C) Pronoun-antecedent agreement. *Everybody* is singular; *our* is plural.
(D) Redundancy. *Own* and *individual* are redundant.

15. (C)
(A) Misplaced modifier. *In her newest cookbook* does not modify *prepare*. Pronoun reference error. The pronoun *her* cannot refer to the possessive noun *Julia Child's*.
(B) Comma splice. Two independent clauses cannot be joined with a comma.
(D) Passive voice. An active construction is preferable.
(E) Dangling participle. The phrase *preparing recipes from her cookbook* does not modify *Julia Child*.

Writing
Chapter 3

Improving Paragraphs

Strategies:

1. Directions for Improving Paragraphs & How the Questions Will Look

2. Combining Two Discrete Sentences

3. Revising Parts of Sentences or Entire Sentences

4. Paragraph Coherence, Development and Organization

> ✓ **Writing – Improving Paragraphs Strategy #1:**
> • **Know How the Questions Will Look**

The third question type on the SAT Writing section is called Improving Paragraphs. The rough draft of a student essay is provided, followed by several questions about how it can be improved. All of the questions follow a multiple-choice format with five answer options, (A) – (E).

> ✓ **Writing – Improving Paragraphs Strategy #2:**
> • **Combine Two Discrete Sentences**

Combining sentences turns simple and short sentences into more meaningful and complex sentences. Combine the same subject(s) and verb(s) whenever possible. Creating complex sentences also shows the relationships among ideas. The goals in sentence combination are to use fewer words overall, to add variety, and to express thoughts more clearly.

The use of a coordinating or subordinating conjunction helps clarify the relationship between two independent clauses in a sentence. Use a coordinating conjunction (*and, but, nor, or, for, so,* and *yet*) to express equally important ideas. A subordinating conjunction (such as *after, although, as, as if, because, before, even though, if, in order that, once, since, so, than, though, unless, until, when, where, whether,* and *while*) joins two independent clauses to show an unequal relationship.

The following paragraph is followed by a sentence combination question:

(1) Existentialism is a philosophy, comprised of different theories, that describes the relationship of the individual to a higher being or to the world. (2) Jean-Paul Sartre was an existentialist. (3) He believed that we are responsible for what we make of ourselves. (4) He did not believe that a higher being forces us to act.

Which sentence is the best combination of sentences 2 and 3 repeated below?

Jean-Paul Sartre was an existentialist. He believed that we are responsible for what we make of ourselves.

(A)   Jean-Paul Sartre was an existentialist, so he believed that we are responsible for what we make of ourselves.

(B)   Although believing that we are responsible for what we make of ourselves, Jean-Paul Sartre was an existentialist.

(C)   Jean-Paul Sartre was an existentialist, but he believed that we are responsible for what we make of ourselves.

(D)   Having been an existentialist, Jean-Paul Sartre believed that we are responsible for what we make of ourselves.

(E)   Jean-Paul Sartre was an existentialist who believed that we are responsible for what we make of ourselves.

First decide the nature of the relationship between the two sentences. Sentence 3 provides a further definition of a term used in sentence 2, *existentialist*. Choice (E) makes this definition clear: *Sartre was an existentialist who....* Choice (A)'s use of *so* and Choice (D)'s use of *having been an existentialist* both incorrectly imply that being an existentialist caused Sartre to formulate his theory. However, it was Sartre's belief in his theory that categorized him as an existentialist. Choices (B) and (C) incorrectly use the conjunctions *although* and *but* respectively.

SENTENCE COMBINATION PRACTICE EXERCISES

Combine each of the following pairs of sentences into one sentence. The new sentence should clearly and accurately express both ideas.

1. Kendal plans to enroll in advanced algebra. She also thinks that she'll take chemistry.

2. Her car broke down on the freeway. She forgot to change the oil.

3. Michelle does her homework at the library. Y Thuan studies at home.

4. Gandhi practiced non-violent protest. Martin Luther King also staged peaceful demonstrations.

5. Cellular phones are very popular. They are small, convenient, and affordable.

Sentence Combination Exercises: Suggested Answers

1. Kendal plans to take both advanced algebra and chemistry. *The subject is the same in both sentences.*

2. Her car broke down on the freeway because she forgot to change the oil. *Adding the word "because" shows the relationship between the two events.*

3. Michelle does her homework at the library while Y Thuan studies at home. *These two phrases can be combined using "while."*

4. Gandhi and Martin Luther King both practiced non-violent protest and staged peaceful demonstrations. *Create one sentence in which the subjects are combined and the similar predicates are combined.*

5. Cellular phones are popular because they are small, convenient, and affordable. *Using the word "because" shows the relationship between the subject and its adjectives.*

> ✓ **Writing – Improving Paragraphs Strategy #3:**
>
> • **Effectively Revise Parts of Sentences or Entire Sentences (Grammar, Clarity & Style)**

Essays may include sentences that lack clarity, contain usage errors, or are expressed ineffectively. Select revisions for these sentences that are concise, clear and grammatically correct. The improved essay should flow smoothly with proper transitions.

The following are types of grammatical errors that are frequently encountered in sentence revision questions:
  • Mismatched pronoun and antecedent
  • Inconsistent verb tense
  • Wrong conjunction

Revision questions may also cover the following flaws in writing style:

- Word repetition, wordiness, or redundancy
- Inappropriate word choice
- Poor transitions
- Awkward constructions
- Reference to material not covered in the essay

Each of the following three paragraphs is followed by a sentence revision question.

(1) Frozen dinners did not come about after freezers were invented. (2) They were made as early as prehistoric times when people in the Arctic naturally preserved foods such as fish. (3) After the 19th century food was also preserved in mixtures of salt and ice. (4) Later Germany employed a method called flash freezing in commercial foods. (5) This method slows down the development of microorganisms by freezing the product rapidly. (6) Frozen foods retain most of their original flavors and forms.

1.   Which is a best way to revise the underlined portion of sentence 2?

They were made as early as prehistoric times when people in the Arctic preserved foods such as fish.

(A)   (correct as it is)
(B)   The time was
(C)   Instead, frozen foods were made
(D)   Freezers were made
(E)   Actually, foods were first frozen

The problem in sentence 2 (restated in choice (A)) is the word *they*. Does the word *they* refer to frozen dinners or to freezers? Choice (B) is a redundant construction that fails to refer directly to frozen foods. Freezers, as we know them today, were not in use during prehistoric times, so choice (D) is incorrect. Choice (C) is a possible answer, but choice (E) is clearer in meaning.

(1) There is no real cure for the common cold. The medicines or treatments we take only suppress the symptoms of a cold. (2) Most people are not aware that colds are viral infections, and they take antibiotics when they shouldn't; antibiotics are effective against bacterial infections only. (3) Consuming vitamin C, our colds sometimes go away. (4) However, research does not support this assumption. (5) The best way to prevent the cold virus is to wash your hands.

2.   Which of the following represents the best construction for sentence 3 (repeated below)?

Consuming vitamin C, our colds sometimes go away.

(A)   (correct as it is)
(B)   Our colds sometimes go away when vitamin C is consumed by us.
(C)   Consuming vitamin C can help us get rid of colds.
(D)   If one consumes vitamin C, their colds often go away.
(E)   When we consume vitamin C, away goes a cold.

The sentence, which is repeated by choice (A), contains a dangling modifier. It sounds as if *colds* are *consuming vitamin C*. Choice (B) presents a passive construction. Choice (D) contains a shift in pronoun number from singular (*one*) to plural (*their*). Choice (E)'s phrase *away goes a cold* is awkwardly ordered. Choice (C) is the best answer.

(1) It is uncertain where and when the sport badminton originated, but its popularity emerged in recent history. (2) The game, similar to tennis, probably originated in India where it was called "Poona." (3) The British officers in India introduced the sport to England when at about 1870 it became known as "battledore" and "shuttlecock." (4) "Badminton" is named after the Duke of Beaufort, who frequently was playing with friends at his estate. (5) England then introduced badminton to the U.S. in the 1890s, where it then became popular in the 1930s. (6) Badminton was recognized as a competitive Olympic sport in 1992.

3.   Which is the best way to revise the underlined portion of sentence 4 (repeated below)?

  "Badminton" is named after the Duke of Beaufort, who frequently <u>was playing</u> with friends at his estate.

(A) (Correct as it is)
(B) is playing
(C) plays
(D) has played
(E) played

Because badminton is *named after the Duke of Beaufort*, it is clear that the duke is a figure from the past. Choice (E) provides the correct past tense verb *played*. Choices (A) – (D) all offer other incorrect verb tense choices.

> ✓ **Writing – Improving Paragraphs Strategy #4:**
> • **Watch for Paragraph Coherence, Development and Organization**

Paragraph organization questions discuss the essay's structure with respect to the argument's development and focus. These types of questions frequently address the following points:
  • Addition or deletion of sentences
  • Organizational scheme and structure
  • Rhetorical devices used
  • Methods of providing specific support
  • Developmental strategies
  • Identification of the main idea

Read the following passage and answer the questions that follow.

(1) While you sleep, your dreams can take on a life of their own. (2) Sometimes you have frightening nightmares that seem real until you wake up. (3) However, in lucid dreams, you can control your dreams because you are conscious that you are dreaming. (4) You can fly through trees, meet someone famous, or be someone else in a lucid dream. (5) Lucid dreaming can be a form of entertainment, but it also can be a self-improvement technique.

(6) Lucid dreaming can help you mentally prepare for important upcoming events. (7) These events can include public performances that require calm confidence and concentration. (8) You can't perform well if you aren't calm

or confident. (9) However, lucid dreaming is not effective in improving physiological or psychological disorders, such as high blood pressure or depression, which should be treated by a health professional.

1.   Which of the following sentences is unnecessary in developing the essay and should be deleted?

(A) Sentence 3
(B) Sentence 5
(C) Sentence 6
(D) Sentence 7
(E) Sentence 8

Answer: (E)

This sentence is implied by the content of sentence 7.

2.   Which of the following sentences would be the most appropriate to add immediately after sentence 7?

(A) For example, anxiety about an upcoming piano recital or speaking engagement can be overcome through lucid dreams.
(B) It is obvious that leaders use lucid dreams to prepare for meetings.
(C) This is a sure way to win any competition, but you must practice.
(D) Lucid dreaming can also occur during short naps as long as the environment is quiet.
(E) Unfortunately you cannot prevent accidents from happening, so do not rely on lucid dreams.

Answer: (A)

Concrete examples *(upcoming piano recital or speaking engagement)* illustrate the abstract idea presented in sentence 7. Specific examples are essential in supporting any abstract or vague concepts.

3.   The author does all of the following EXCEPT

(A) provide examples to illustrate a point
(B) identify more than one possible benefit
(C) address opposing viewpoints
(D) recognize a limitation
(E) contrast like yet dissimilar experiences

Answer: (C)

The author does not include any opposing views in the essay. Choice (A) can be found in sentence 4: *You can fly through trees, meet someone famous, or be someone else in a lucid dream.* Choice (B) is present in sentence 5: *Lucid dreaming can be a form of entertainment, but it also can be a self-improvement technique.* Choice (D) is apparent in the final sentence: *However, lucid dreaming is not effective in improving physiological or psychological disorders, such as high blood pressure or depression, which should be treated by a health professional.* Finally, Choice (E) is evidenced by sentences 1 and 2, which contrast the turmoil of nightmares with the freedom of lucid dreaming.

IMPROVING PARAGRAPHS
PRACTICE EXERCISES

(1) Although most students still attend school, a lot of students are now taking up the opportunity of home schooling. (2) Even though home schooling has been around for a long time, it has become really popular lately. (3) A lot of famous people have been home schooled. (4) More and more we are going to have to get used to home schooling.

(5) Home schooling is in vogue for a bunch of different reasons. (6) Parents want more control over their students' academics. (7) They also want to pick courses that may not be offered by the local schools. (8) Parents can include hard subjects that aren't offered at school, like advanced literature, math, logic and other demanding subjects. (9) Home school supporters say that students get to learn at their own pace. (10) Many students with demanding athletic, dramatic or other activities require a flexible academic schedule to accommodate these activities. (11) Parents choose home schooling because it offers the opportunity for more field trips, like to factories and musical events. (12) Home-schooled students are not exposed to on-campus problems such as drugs, violence, and peer pressure. (13) Students probably do not take drugs if they are at home during the day.

(14) Although home schooling has become widespread, many people still question whether or not it is as effective as regular school. (15) Opponents of home schooling say that it doesn't offer students the opportunity to get together with their own age group. (16) Home-schooled students don't have to cooperate or compete like you have to at school. (17) They might not be good at getting and keeping jobs because they did school as a solo act and they don't know how to work together. (18) There is no structure at home so you don't really know what to study and when.

(19) Home schooling is not the same as real school. (20) Anyone can see that, whether they agree with home schooling or not. (21) Motivated students probably do okay learning things at home, but other students need more structure. (22) There is a danger that you could end up watching too much TV, so it is really up to the self-discipline of the student.

1. Which is the best revision of the underlined portion of sentence 1 (repeated below)?

    Although most students still attend regular school, <u>a lot of students are now taking up the opportunity of home schooling.</u>

(A) the opportunity of home schooling is now being taken by a lot of students.
(B) a growing number of students now prefers the home schooling alternative.
(C) there is getting to be a large number of home-schooled students.
(D) others don't.
(E) other students preferring home schooling as an alternative.

2. To improve the coherence of the second paragraph, which sentence would it best to delete?

(A) Sentence 5
(B) Sentence 6
(C) Sentence 9
(D) Sentence 12
(E) Sentence 13

3. Taking into account the content of paragraph 2, which of the following is the best revision of the paragraph's topic sentence (sentence 5)?

(A) Home schooling has become a popular educational alternative for a wide variety of reasons.
(B) The many reasons that home schooling is popular are too many to state.
(C) Popular as an alternative to regular school, some students like home schooling better.
(D) The superiority of home schooling to regular schooling is well documented, students perform better academically.
(E) In comparing regular schooling and home schooling, many feel that home schooling is the best choice.

4. Which of the following is the best way to combine sentences 6 and 7 (repeated below)?

Parents want more control over their students' academics. They also want to pick courses that may not be offered by the local schools.

(A) Parents want more control over their students' academics and to pick different courses than what the schools offer.
(B) Parents wanting control over their students' academics are also wanting to pick different courses than what the schools offer.
(C) Parents want to control their students' academics and to select courses not offered at local schools.
(D) Parents, wanting more control over their students' academics, to pick different courses than what the schools offer.
(E) Parents wanting more control over their students' academics, picking different courses than what the school offers.

5. Which of the following could be added to improve sentence 3?

A lot of famous people have been home schooled.

(A) indicate the year that the first famous person was home-schooled
(B) explain why some famous people were home-schooled
(C) indicate that common people are also home-schooled
(D) provide examples of famous home-schooled students
(E) list popular subjects that famous people studied

6. The author does all of the following EXCEPT:

(A) support an assertion
(B) provide a personal anecdote to make a point
(C) describe a potential negative outcome
(D) develop an argument with pros and cons
(E) illustrate a point with specific examples

Answer Explanations

1.   (B)

(A)   Passive construction.
(C)   Awkward construction.
(D)   Does not convey the full meaning of the sentence, as it includes nothing about home schooling.
(E)   Sentence fragment lacking a main verb.

2.   (E)

All sentences except 13 provide reasons for home schooling. Sentence 13 departs from the subject.

3.   (A)

(B)   Awkwardly expressed, wordy and redundant.
(C)   Dangling participle. *Popular as an alternative to regular school* modifies *home schooling,* not *students.*
(D)   Comma splice. A comma may not separate two independent clauses.
(E)   Comparative degree. Use *better* in comparing two choices instead of *best.*

4.   (C)

(A)   Wordy construction not in parallel form.
(B)   Wordy and awkward construction.
(D)   Mixed construction.
(E)   Sentence fragment.

5.   (D)

Providing specific examples of famous people who have been home schooled would best expand the existing sentence and build reader interest.

6.   (B)

(A)   The second paragraph supports the assertion made in topic sentence 5, and the third paragraph supports the assertion made in topic sentence 14.
(C)   The potential negative results of home schooling are addressed in the third paragraph.
(D)   The essay presents a pro-con argument about home schooling.
(E)   Sentences 11 and 12 both include specific examples.

Writing
Chapter 4

The Essay

Overview:

Introduction to the SAT Essay

Strategies:

1. Understand the SAT Essay Prompts & Write About the Stated Topic
2. The Three Steps to Writing a Successful SAT Essay
3. Understand the 5-Paragraph and 3-Paragraph Essay Formats
4. Write Enough
5. Provide Adequate Supporting Details
6. Organize and Develop Your Essay
7. Use Effective Transitions
8. Improve Your Writing Skills
9. Five Paragraph Essay Outline
10. SAT Essay Checklist
11. Understand Holistic Scoring
12. Notes from an SAT Essay Evaluator
13. Sample SAT Essays
14. Practice Essay Prompts

Reference:

SAT Essay Score Chart

The Essay on the SAT

Essay Overview

The SAT includes a 25-minute written essay. The purpose of the essay is to evaluate a student's ability to write on demand without the assistance of a teacher, tutor, friend, parent, or computer tools such as spelling and grammar checks. The 25-minute essay is a component within a 50-minute SAT Writing section; the remaining 25 minutes are dedicated to multiple-choice grammar questions.

The SAT essay counts for approximately 1/3 of the 800 points available in the total SAT writing score. Rather than simply consider SAT Writing scores, college admissions officials can opt to review actual essays.

The essay is written in response to a specific question or prompt. It is important to address the prompt as stated and to provide detailed examples and reasons to support your position. The amount of time will not allow you to write a refined, final essay. Your goal should be to provide a logical, developed and well-organized preliminary draft.

The SAT essay is scored holistically, which means that it is evaluated based on the overall impression that it makes. One evaluator likened the essay scoring process to judging stew at a county fair. The meat, sauce, herbs, and vegetables are not evaluated separately – the whole stew is judged. Essay graders focus upon the essay's demonstration of critical thinking, development, and use of language. Grammar, usage, and mechanics are not the main consideration in determining an essay's score, but they contribute to the perceived quality of the essay. Word choice, diction, organization, and the presence of detailed support are also factors that affect the essay's general impact. Penmanship is not to be considered unless the essay is unreadable, but neatness is obviously an asset in the overall presentation.

If writing the SAT essay seems daunting to you, take heart. SAT essay scorers understand that writing an essay under such demanding time constraints with no outside resources available is very difficult for students. Essay readers are supposed to take a positive approach in scoring essays, focusing upon what has been included in the essay, not what has been left out.

✓ **Writing – Essay Strategy #1:**
• **Know the Nature of the SAT Essay Prompts**
• **Write About the Stated Topic**

On the SAT, you will be expected to write an essay in which you state your position or opinion about a particular issue and then provide appropriate support for your argument. SAT writing prompts are often famous quotes, observations or general philosophical statements with which you are asked to agree or disagree in a persuasive or argumentative essay. Here are two examples of SAT essay prompts:

Sample Essay Prompt #1:

The famous writer George Bernard Shaw noted: "Progress is impossible without change, and those who cannot change their minds cannot change anything."

What is your opinion about the concept that progress is impossible without change, and that the ability to change one's mind is an essential factor in changing anything else? Write an essay addressing this topic and your point of view about it. Provide support for your position with examples and reasoning drawn from your personal experience or what you have learned through your reading, schoolwork, and observations.

Sample Essay Prompt #2:

Robert Frost wrote:
"Two roads diverged in a wood, and I –
I took the one less traveled by,
And that has made all the difference."

It has been said that our lives are largely the result of a series of choices we have made, some of which are associated with taking significant risks. Discuss an important choice (made by you or by someone else) that involved taking a risk. What effect did this decision have? What do you believe would have been the result if a different choice had been made?

It is very important that you carefully read and respond to the essay prompt provided. Your essay must address the topic as stated. Essays written on subjects other than the topic assigned will receive a score of zero. Write the best essay you can in response to the essay prompt provided.

> ✓ **Writing – Essay Strategy #2:**
>
> • **The Three Steps to Writing a Successful SAT Essay**

If the doctor told me I had six minutes to live, I'd type a little faster.

– Isaac Asimov

Twenty-five minutes is not much time to write an essay, so it is vital that you use the time available to your best advantage. **There are three steps in writing a quality SAT essay: plan, write and proofread. Time must be managed carefully in completing each step.**

1.   PLAN (2 – 3 minutes):
Carefully read the essay prompt and quickly decide how you plan to respond to it. Identify the main point you want to make with respect to the stated assignment. Summarize this main point in the margin of your test booklet. Spend about two to three minutes brainstorming. Jot down examples, reasons and other ideas that will support or develop your point. Cluster your ideas with a spoke outline (the central idea at the center and "spokes" drawn out to supporting ideas) or with a standard concept outline.

Here is a "spoke outline" for the sample essay prompt #1 stated above about change and progress:

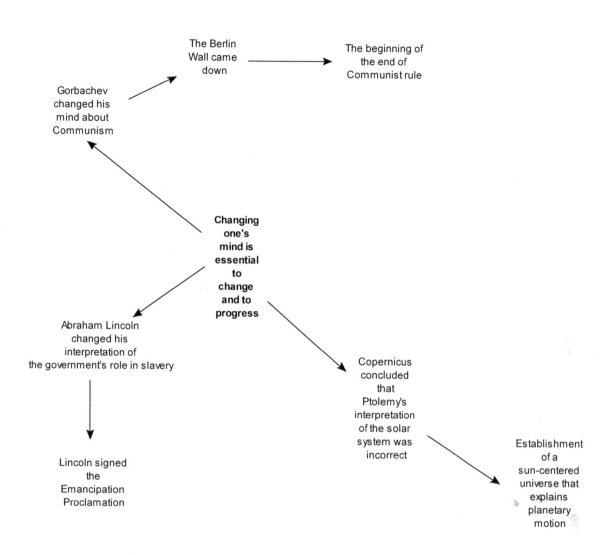

Here is a rough concept outline for sample essay prompt #2 stated above about an important choice:

- Joined the tennis team in 10th grade:
  - Got in shape
  - Made friends
  - Built self-confidence
  - Won Athlete of the Month/MVP awards
  - Learned commitment and responsibility

- If I hadn't:
  - Inactive
  - Lonely
  - Poor self-esteem

2.   WRITE (20 minutes)

Provide an introduction, one-to-three body paragraphs, and a conclusion (see the next section for details about formatting, etc.). Write what you know about the topic with an authentic voice. Do not pretend to be someone you are not. It is a mistake to invent life experiences to fit the essay. Be yourself on paper. Write with feeling and conviction.

3.   PROOFREAD (2 – 3 minutes)

Carefully read over your essay for grammatical and spelling errors. Neatly make any corrections needed by carefully erasing or by using crisp, single-line cross-outs for words you wish to omit or change.

✓ **Writing – Essay Strategy #3:**

• **Understand the 5-Paragraph and 3-Paragraph Essay Formats**

Although it is not the required format for the SAT essay, the five-paragraph essay may be the best format for you to follow on your particular essay assignment. The five-paragraph essay consists of an introductory paragraph, three body paragraphs, and a concluding paragraph. A three-paragraph essay format can also be used; in this case, one strong middle paragraph replaces the three body paragraphs.

The Introductory Paragraph

The introductory paragraph invites the reader into the essay and announces the point that the writer intends to make or prove. The balance of a successful essay provides the proof. The essay's main idea is clearly presented in a thesis statement. A good introductory paragraph will make it clear that you understood and are responding to the essay prompt or assignment. The evaluator should be certain that you understood the prompt and plan to fully address it. You may choose to open your introductory paragraph with an intriguing opening line or "hook" intended to capture the reader's interest. If you do so, make sure that you exercise good judgment; do not make casual or bizarre opening statements that could be off-putting to the essay reader.

Your thesis statement should include three subtopics that correspond to the three central paragraphs of your essay. The first subtopic in the thesis statement is the kernel of the first body paragraph's topic sentence, the second subtopic is presented in the topic sentence of the second body paragraph, and the third subtopic is re-stated in the third body paragraph's topic sentence. A thesis statement developed from the spoke outline above regarding change and progress might read as follows:

> Great minds that have changed and thus caused the world to change include those of the astronomer Copernicus, whose changed mind led scientists to reevaluate the center of the solar system, Abraham Lincoln, who reversed his interpretation of the government's role and emancipated slaves, and Mikhail Gorbachev, who changed his view of Communism and set free millions of oppressed people.

Central Paragraphs

The three central paragraphs are used to expand upon the three subtopics stated in the thesis. Each body paragraph will open with a topic sentence derived from one of these three subtopics. The three subtopics in the thesis statement above are as follows:

1. Copernicus, whose changed mind led scientists to reevaluate the center of the solar system

2. Abraham Lincoln, who reversed his interpretation of the government's role and emancipated slaves

3. Mikhail Gorbachev, who changed his view of Communism and set free millions of oppressed people

The opening topic sentences for each of the paragraphs will be derived directly from each subtopic. The topic sentences for the three body paragraphs corresponding to the above subtopics might be as follows:

➢ *Topic sentence for body paragraph 1:*
The revolutionary 16th century astronomer Copernicus did not have as much trouble changing his own mind as he did changing everyone else's.

➢ *Topic sentence for body paragraph 2:*
Like Copernicus, Abraham Lincoln changed his mind about an important issue and tremendous controversy erupted.

➢ *Topic sentence for body paragraph 3:*
Mikhail Gorbachev became a modern-day Lincoln when he changed his mind about continuing to support Communism and freed the people of Russia and Eastern Europe living under Communist rule.

The body paragraphs' topic sentences are each followed by two to four support sentences that further develop and expand upon the point made in the topic sentence. These support sentences may elaborate upon, substantiate, or reinforce the topic sentence with more specific details, reasons, facts, evidence, statistics, examples, reports, expert or personal testimony, or quotations.

Conclusion

The conclusion of the essay provides a recap of the concepts and ideas stated in the essay. It re-states the thesis and reiterates key points and arguments. The conclusion depends upon the content of the introductory and body paragraphs; choosing strong thesis statement subtopics, presenting these ideas in a logical sequence, and providing detailed support for them in the body paragraphs of your essay will contribute to your ability to write a strong concluding paragraph.

In the conclusion, you may draw reasonable inferences based upon evidence presented in the body paragraphs. The conclusion should be a focused closing that revisits the essay's key points and arguments and summarizes your point of view. You may make reference to an important related topic that is outside of the scope of the essay at hand. Ending with a memorable quote or phrase or an intriguing concept will make a significant final impression upon the reader.

ALTERNATIVE FORMATS

If you do not think you can write an adequate 5-paragraph essay in the time allowed, you may choose instead to write a 3- or 4-paragraph essay. In a 3-paragraph essay, for example, your thesis contains one main idea that is expanded upon in the middle or single body paragraph.

✓ **Writing – Essay Strategy #4:**

• **Write Enough**

Use the full time allotted (25 minutes) to write a well-developed essay. It is important to write enough to make a favorable impression upon the reader. It is not enough to write a few good lines; you must be able to develop and expand upon your main point with enough supporting details to show that you have command of the topic. Your essay should reflect skillful use of vocabulary and varied sentence structure; these features are not made apparent in just a few sentences. It should be your goal to write a three-to-five paragraph essay without padding it with repetitive or reworked ideas.

✓ **Writing – Essay Strategy #5:**

• **Provide Adequate Supporting Details**

---

*Most of the basic material a writer works with is acquired
before the age of fifteen.*

– Willa Cather

Illustrative examples for your SAT essay may be drawn from history or literature, but also from current events, science, art, music, film, modern culture, sports and personal experience. The important factor is to use the examples well. When expanding upon the topic sentence, write with as much precision and with as much detail as possible. In the essay topic stated above regarding change and progress, the examples are provided by science, history and recent current events.

Personal experience remains an excellent source for supporting evidence and examples. If you choose to relate an incident from your past, remember that the SAT essay evaluators are more interested in the quality and style of your composition than in the nature or importance of the events you write about. Make past experiences come to life with vivid details that cover who, what, where, when and why. Use clear and expressive language. Stay focused on the main point of your story and do not digress. Remember why you are recounting an event: to respond to the essay prompt in a meaningful way.

Here is an example of how to expand upon a topic sentence to create a well-developed body paragraph. This first body paragraph for the previously stated essay prompt regarding change includes appropriate supporting details:

> The 16th century astronomer Copernicus did not have as much trouble changing his own mind as he did changing everyone else's. Copernicus and his peers conceived of a universe based upon the observations of Ptolemy, a Greek astronomer who believed that the sun and planets revolve around the earth. Copernicus came to conclude that Ptolemy's interpretation was wrong, and he introduced the controversial concept of a sun-centered universe. Copernicus changed his view and, as a result, the center of the solar system became known to be the sun, marking the beginning of a scientific revolution.

✓ **Writing – Essay Strategy #6:**

• **Organize and Develop Your Essay**

Stories have a beginning, a middle and an end. But not necessarily in that order.

– Robert Silverberg

When you first establish the ideas you intend to incorporate in your essay (the three subtopics of your thesis statement), spend a moment to decide the order in which they should be presented. The paragraphs should be sequenced effectively. They can be organized by relative importance, in which case your points should be made in the following order:

First body paragraph:	2nd most significant point
Second body paragraph:	3rd most significant point
Third body paragraph:	Most significant point of the three

If supporting examples are taken from the past, you may choose to sequence them chronologically. The essay in progress regarding change presents examples in order from the least recent to the most recent: first Copernicus, then Abraham Lincoln, and finally Mikhail Gorbachev.

Arrange the sentences within your paragraphs in the most effective order. One sentence should flow easily into the next, and subsequent material should elaborate upon previous statements. Do not jump from one idea to another. Ideas should be connected with smooth transitions.

✓ **Writing – Essay Strategy #7:**

• **Use Effective Transitions**

Effective transitions between sentences and paragraphs enhance an essay's organization, coherence and flow.

Transitions Between Sentences: Use transitional words or phrases between sentences to logically and effectively advance the text and develop arguments.

Transitions Between Paragraphs: The first sentence of a paragraph should make reference to material contained in the previous paragraph and show how the current paragraph will further build and expand upon what has come before.

Here is an example for the essay in progress:

Like Copernicus, Abraham Lincoln changed his mind about an important issue and tremendous controversy erupted.

The opening words *Like Copernicus* refer to the topic of the previous paragraph. The topic sentence goes on to compare Lincoln's situation with that of Copernicus.

Use of the following words and phrases provide effective transitions from one part of the essay to the next:

PURPOSE OF TRANSITION	POSSIBLE TRANSITIONAL WORD OR PHRASE:
To further develop ideas or add new ideas or information	Additionally, Further, Also
To introduce specific examples	For instance, For example, To illustrate this point
To provide details about location or setting	Above, Below, Adjacent to, Here, There
To provide sequence	First, Second, Then, Next, Finally, Lastly
To advance forward or backward in time	Before, Previously, During, Meanwhile, Later, Subsequently, Eventually
To compare or contrast previous text	But, Although, Nevertheless, On the contrary, Likewise, Similarly, In comparison
To emphasize or clarify a point just made	Of course, In other words, Obviously, Undoubtedly
To refer to a point made earlier	As previously mentioned, As noted earlier
To announce a result, effect, or summarizing statement	So, As a result, Consequently, Therefore, Thus
To introduce a final concluding statement	Accordingly, In summary, Overall, In conclusion

The following second body paragraph of the essay in progress reflects the use of transitional words and phrases *(italicized)*:

> *Like Copernicus,* Abraham Lincoln changed his mind about an important issue and tremendous controversy erupted. *Before* he took office and during his first year as president, Lincoln thought that the Constitution did not allow for the chief executive to put an end to slavery. *But* Lincoln changed his mind about the role of the government in the abolition of slavery. *Thus,* in 1862 Lincoln signed the Emancipation Proclamation, putting an end to a terrible and regrettable practice. *Although* his decision was met with serious opposition, it later was viewed as one of his crowning achievements.

✓ **Writing – Essay Strategy #8:**
• **Improve Your Writing Skills**

Verbs are the most important of all your tools. They push the sentence
forward to give it momentum. Active verbs push hard; passive verbs tug fitfully.

– William Zinsser

1.   **Use Active Rather than Passive Verb Forms.** *Example:*

PASSIVE VOICE: An increase in vitamin intake among professional athletes *was observed* by nutritionists.

ACTIVE VOICE: Nutritionists *observed* an increase in vitamin intake among professional athletes.

In passive sentences, the subject receives the action. In active sentences, the subject performs the action. Active constructions are stronger, livelier, shorter, and easier to read than passive constructions.

2.   **Use Coordination to Relate Ideas of Equal Emphasis**

Use coordinating conjunctions (*and, but, nor, or, for, so* and *yet*) or use a semi-colon accompanied by a conjunctive adverb (*however, moreover,* or *therefore*) to present two different but equally important ideas in one sentence. *Examples:*

> Aunt Kay took Simon to the Space Needle, *and* she bought him a souvenir in the gift shop.

> We thought the game started at 1:00 p.m., *but* it really started at 2:00 p.m.

> Uncle Ken just fed the llamas; *however,* in an hour they will be hungry again.

3.   **Use Subordination to Add Emphasis to One of the Ideas**

Subordination allows the writer to distinguish between main ideas and less important, or "subordinate" ideas. Subordination permits the introduction and addition of details and establishing a logical relationship between ideas. Subordinate clauses contain the less important information and usually begin with a subordinating conjunction or relative pronoun.

Subordinating conjunctions (not all are listed)**:** *after, although, as, as if, because, before, even though, if, in order that, once, since, so, than, though, unless, until, when, where, whether, while*

Relative pronouns: *that, which, who, whom, whose*

Examples:

> *Because* she had never been abroad, Bridget was particularly excited to go to Ireland.

> The benefit was held at the St. Regis Resort in Monarch Beach, *which* is a popular local vacation spot.

4.   Use Specific Rather than General Language.

Use appropriate adjectives to modify nouns and adverbs to modify adjectives, verbs and other adverbs. *Example:*

> The boat entered the harbor.

Here are two completely different scenarios that expand and improve upon this sentence with descriptive detail:

- Gleaming in the sunlight, the modern ocean liner steamed into the quaint marina as its passengers cavorted on deck.

- The depleted vessel, its tattered sails fluttering briskly in the wind, tottered into the port's sanctuary just before sundown.

5.   Turn Assertions into Arguments: An assertion is a statement, while an argument must be supported by facts or logic. Use the word *because* to introduce supporting reasons.

Assertion: *Los Angeles is a great place to vacation.*

Argument: *Los Angeles is a great place to vacation because it has excellent beaches, famous Hollywood sites, and unparalleled amusement parks.*

SUPPORTED Argument: *Los Angeles is a great place to vacation because it has excellent beaches such as Malibu and Venice, famous Hollywood sites including Grauman's Chinese Theatre and the Sunset Strip, and unparalleled amusement parks ranging from Disneyland to Knott's Berry Farm.*

6.   Avoid Logical Fallacies in Arguments.

- **False Cause:** Just because one event happens after another does not mean that the first event caused the second to occur. Causal relationships between phenomena requires substantive evidence; causation is more than mere correlation. *Example:*

> After eating oatmeal for breakfast for several years, my cousin gave birth to triplets. Therefore, eating oatmeal caused my cousin to bear triplets.

- **Hasty Generalization:** A generalization derived from an insufficient sample. *Example:*

> I was served a flavorless sandwich at a café in Paris. All of the food in Paris must be unsavory.

- **Circular Reasoning (Begging the Question):** The conclusion of the argument is the support of the premise; what you are supposed to be proving is assumed to be true. *Example:*

  > All of Rembrandt's paintings are artistic masterpieces. Artistic masterpieces are produced only by great painters, so Rembrandt was a great painter because all of his paintings are artistic masterpieces.

- **Emotive Language:** Use of language intended to stimulate emotions is not a substitute for a successful argument. *Example:*

  > The general is a military oppressor addicted to instigating heinous wars that mutilate innocent civilians.

Writers should also avoid exaggeration or persuasive speech in place of supported arguments.

EXAGGERATION: If we all don't get flu shots then students will miss weeks of school and employees will take so many sick days that the economy will start to fail.

PERSUASIVE SPEECH: If you do not want to spend several days in bed sick and miserable with terrible aches, pains and nausea, you had better get a flu shot.

SUPPORTED ARGUMENT: The strain of this year's flu is particularly virulent, and because it has already advanced from Asia to North America, it is important to get a flu shot. (The supported argument rather persuasive language reflects the urgency of the situation.)

The following shows the third body paragraph of the essay in progress. Its sentences reflect the use of active constructions, coordination, subordination, specific language and other writing techniques outlined in this section *(coordinating conjunctions, subordinating conjunctions and relative pronouns are italicized):*

> Mikhail Gorbachev became a modern-day Lincoln when he changed his mind about continuing to support Communism *and* freed the people of Russia and Eastern Europe living under Communist rule. *Because* he was entrenched in the Cold War politics of his predecessors, Gorbachev did not initially try to overturn Communism. *Once* he had had the opportunity to travel his country and the world, Gorbachev became convinced of the tremendous struggle of the oppressed Russian people. *When* Gorbachev saw how much his citizenry was suffering, he decided that Communism had reached its end. A wave of democracy swept Eastern Europe, *and* the Berlin Wall fell. The old Soviet Union and its Eastern European satellites are no more *because* Mikhail Gorbachev changed his mind about continuing to support Communism.

The essay's conclusion is made forceful through a series of short, emphatic sentences:

> Good men stand by their principles. Great men change their minds and change the world. The sun is the known center of the universe. Slaves are free. Communism is over. People with courage have strong convictions. Those with even greater courage have changed their convictions to better the world in which we live.

✓ **Writing – Essay Strategy #9:**

• **Practice with the Five Paragraph Essay Outline**

Essay Prompt: _____

_____

_____

Introduction

Thesis Statement: _____

_____

/when/because/as a result of/are/are demonstrated by/are shown by/

(Subtopic 1): _____

_____,

(Subtopic 2): _____

_____, and

(Subtopic 3): _____

_____.

Body Paragraphs

(First Body Paragraph)

Topic Sentence from Subtopic 1 of Thesis: _____

_____

_____.

1st Support Sentence: _____

_____.

2nd Support Sentence: _____

_____.

3rd Support Sentence: _____

_____.

(Second Body Paragraph)

Topic Sentence from Subtopic 2 of Thesis: _____

_____

_____.

1st Support Sentence: _____

_____.

2nd Support Sentence: _____

_____.

3rd Support Sentence: _____

_____.

(Third Body Paragraph)

Topic Sentence from Subtopic 3 of Thesis: _____

_____

_____.

1st Support Sentence: _____

_____.

2nd Support Sentence: _____

_____.

3rd Support Sentence: _____

_____.

Conclusion

(Restate thesis)

_____

_____

_____

_____

✓ **Writing – Essay Strategy #10:**

• **SAT Essay Checklist**

Introduction:
  - ✓ Does the essay respond to the prompt provided?
  - ✓ Does the introduction include an interesting quote, fact, or thought?
  - ✓ Is the thesis statement unified, limited and specific?

Central Paragraphs:
  - ✓ Is a topic sentence provided for each central paragraph?
  - ✓ Is each topic sentence followed by at least 3 – 4 supporting sentences per paragraph?
  - ✓ Are the sentences arranged in the best possible order?
  - ✓ Are the paragraphs effectively sequenced?

Conclusion:
  - ✓ Is the thesis appropriately summarized?
  - ✓ Does the essay end on a thought-provoking point, quote, or question that relates to the original thesis?

Writing:
  - ✓ Does the essay include appropriate transitional words and phrases?
  - ✓ Is the vocabulary appropriate, including use of specific, descriptive language?
  - ✓ Are subordination and coordination used to expand shorter sentences?
  - ✓ Are the arguments free of logical fallacies?
  - ✓ Is the essay long enough?

✓ **Writing – Essay Strategy #11:**

• **Understand Holistic Scoring**

SAT essays are graded holistically; the overall impression of the essay is more important than its individual parts. Holistic scoring allows readers to view an essay as an entire work instead of as individual components. Trained and qualified high school and college instructors score the essays. Two people evaluate each essay. To make grading fair, scorers are not able to view students' names, schools, or each other's scores. The essays are scored on a scale of 1 – 6, 6 being the highest score available. The essay-scoring chart that appears at the end of this chapter provides further details for each score value.

The official readers consider an essay's display of critical thinking, use of language, and expansive development. The combination of separate elements such as diction, incorporation of examples, organization, and grammar all help to determine an essay's holistic value. Holistic evaluation is intended to insure a standard of impartiality and consistency.

Your essay will be evaluated with respect to other essays, not in comparison with an ideal essay. Essay evaluators are instructed to remember that there are ranges within a score; for example, you may have a high, middle, or low "3," but you will still receive a "3" for the essay. Evaluators are also aware that a well-developed essay may not have a fully stated conclusion because the student had only 25 minutes to write the essay.

The evaluator is supposed to bear in mind that the essays are written by high school students, and essays with some errors may still receive a "6" score. All essays will be scored; you will receive a "0" only if you do not address the given topic. Although you may not have had significant exposure with respect to the topic, the reader will look for a logical argument relevant to the issue.

✔ **Writing – Essay Strategy #12:**
• **Implement Some Advice from an SAT Essay Evaluator**

Inside Tips from an SAT Essay Evaluator

I am an official SAT essay evaluator. I have to read and score 200 SAT essays a day for the next three weeks. I have two minutes for yours. I am going to quickly check your essay for the following:

Anatomy of an SAT Essay

A heart: Does your essay have a thesis? A main idea should pulse throughout your essay.
Chambers of the heart: Is your thesis developed with appropriate subtopics?
Bones: Does your essay have a skeleton? It should be structurally and organizationally sound.
Flesh: Are supporting details used to support your argument?
Nerves: Are your reflexes present? "Reflexes" come from your self-correcting message center; they help you select appropriate vocabulary, sentence variety, and essay tone.
Breath: Is there life in your essay? Write with commitment and passion. If you do so, you will automatically write a stronger, more focused, and organized essay.

Dull Essay Prompt…Dull Essay?

Do you think you have dull essay prompt? Even a seemingly insignificant item can prompt great writing. Kafka took a lowly cockroach as his subject and wrote *The Metamorphosis.*

So, do not let an essay prompt push you around! It may be dull or uninteresting to you, but you need not be limited by it. The same paints that a child uses were used by Michelangelo to paint the masterpieces adorning the Sistine Chapel. The tools we use and the essay prompts provided do not matter as much as our mastery of them.

Write with clarity and conviction. Write about what really matters to you and you will naturally be more focused, detailed, and organized.

Care About What You Write and Write About What's Important to You

Most people have greater writing ability than they realize. Whenever I have seen people write about what they truly care about, the level of writing seems to soar – whether it is at the elementary, junior high, high school, or university level.

Pre-Writing: The Easy Way to Get Ideas

Ideas are all around you and also within you. Quickly organize your essay organized by jotting down your main points. Using the following common real life example, you can see how easy it is to develop this process. *Example:*

> Think of yourself as a 16-year-old who wants to borrow your parents' car. List as many reasons as possible why you should be awarded the car for the evening. You can probably rattle off a series of reasons: *I keep my grades up, I'm a good kid, I'm a good driver, last time I borrowed the car there was no problem, I can run errands for you while I'm out, I can take a younger brother or sister en route so you won't need to, I'll baby-sit next weekend, I'll wash or detail the car, I'll get my friend to put in new spark plugs, etc.*

Organize & Sequence Your Ideas

Continuing with the car metaphor, you know that in order to start driving a car you first must turn the key in the ignition. Next you release the emergency brake and put the car in gear. Then you press your foot down on the gas pedal. You may turn on the windshield wipers if it is raining. At some point you will probably turn on the radio or put in a CD. Some of these actions are essential in starting and then driving a car and must be performed in the correct sequence; other items, such as turning on the radio, are incidental and do not move the car forward.

You can benefit from thinking of your essay in the same way. Having generated a series of reasons in the above example, you need to organize them by categories: good kid, good grades, good driver, and other side benefits. These subtopics would actually help you build your thesis statement.

Basically you want to organize your ideas into categories; some writing instructors call this process "clustering." Work in the manner that best suits you whether you cluster your topics in visual groups or use a more formal topic outline.

The Backwards Thesis: Your Secret SAT Essay Ace

Many a great writer has gotten to the end of an essay only to find the original thesis needs changing or refining. Why? Because writing is actually a form of thinking. Through the process of writing, we actually strengthen our thinking and refine our ideas.

Write your essay from the beginning if you prefer. Using this method, you would assert your thesis and its subtopics. However, some students do not even know what their thesis is until they have jotted down and organized a few of their major and minor points.

Write the essay backwards if that works better for you. You can do this by using your "clustering" or major/minor idea outline to provide the very sub-topics that you will actually form into your thesis. **Always put your thesis at the beginning of your SAT essay.** An evaluator will be looking for this vital item that generates the power of your essay. Every essay needs a heart!

The Power of Practice

A few practice writing sessions under timed conditions will give you a vital sense of your own pacing. It will be well worth it to you to practice in simulated test conditions.

<u>**Get a Smart Start!**</u>

Einstein may have proved the relativity of time, but time for the SAT essay will go relatively quickly. **Stay to this formula: Spend only 2-3 minutes jotting down your main ideas.** Form your thesis and support your subtopics with relevant ideas and examples. Use quotes if you can, as evaluators like them. Incorporate examples from your life, history, art, science and other areas of interest. Include as many good supporting points as possible. Remember, you will only be scored on the ideas that make it into the paper. Write quickly. Write effectively. Write with your pencil, your mind, and your heart!

✓ **Writing – Essay Strategy # 13:**

• **Know What Differently Scored Essays Look Like**

Level "6," "4" and "2" essays follow for the two sample essay prompts discussed in this chapter.

Sample Essay Prompt #1:

The famous writer George Bernard Shaw noted: "Progress is impossible without change, and those who cannot change their minds cannot change anything."

What is your opinion about the concept that progress is impossible without change, and that the ability to change one's mind is an essential factor in changing anything else? Write an essay addressing this topic and your point of view about it. Provide support for your position with examples and reasoning drawn from your personal experience or what you have learned through your reading, schoolwork, and observations.

Level "6" essay for this topic:

The great author George Bernard Shaw observed: "Progress is impossible without change, and those who cannot change their minds cannot change anything." Some people believe that a leader will appear weak if he changes his mind about an important matter. While it is important to be steadfast in one's convictions, it is equally important to be able to reconsider one's position and make changes when appropriate. Great minds that have changed and thus caused the world to change include those of the astronomer Copernicus, whose changed mind led scientists to reevaluate the center of the solar system, Abraham Lincoln, who reversed his interpretation of the government's role and emancipated slaves, and Mikhail Gorbachev, who changed his view of Communism and set free millions of oppressed people.

The 16th century astronomer Copernicus did not have as much trouble changing his own mind as he did changing everyone else's. Copernicus and his peers conceived of a universe based upon the observations of Ptolemy, a Greek astronomer who believed that the sun and planets revolve around the earth. Copernicus came to conclude that Ptolemy's interpretation was wrong, and he introduced the controversial concept of a sun-centered universe. Copernicus changed his view and, as a result, the center of the solar system became known to be the sun, marking the beginning of a scientific revolution.

Like Copernicus, Abraham Lincoln changed his mind about an important issue and tremendous controversy erupted. Before he took office and during his first year as president, Lincoln thought that the Constitution did not allow for the chief executive to put an end to slavery. But Lincoln changed his mind about the role of the government in the abolition of slavery. Thus, in 1862 Lincoln signed the Emancipation Proclamation, putting an end to a terrible and regrettable practice. Although his decision was met with serious opposition, it later was viewed as one of his crowning achievements.

Mikhail Gorbachev became a modern-day Lincoln when he changed his mind about continuing to support Communism and freed the people of Russia and Eastern Europe living under Communist rule. Because he was entrenched in the Cold War politics of his predecessors, Gorbachev did not initially try to overturn Communism. Once he had had the opportunity to travel his country and the world, Gorbachev became convinced of the tremendous struggle of the oppressed Russian people. When Gorbachev saw how much his citizenry was suffering, he decided that Communism had reached its end. A wave of democracy swept Eastern Europe, and the Berlin Wall fell. The old Soviet Union and its Eastern European satellites are no more because Mikhail Gorbachev changed his mind about continuing to support Communism.

Good men stand by their principles. Great men change their minds and change the world. The sun is the known center of the universe. Slaves are free. Communism has given way to democracy throughout almost all of the world. People with courage have strong convictions. Those with even greater courage have changed their convictions to better the world in which we live.

This is a level "6" essay. It fully addresses the assigned essay prompt, and its ideas are developed from a strong thesis statement. The argument is well supported with suitable examples and detail. Sentences are clearly constructed and reflect appropriate vocabulary and transitional language. The writer has observed the conventions of standard written English.

Level "4" essay for the same topic:

The great author George Bernard Shaw observed: "Progress is impossible without change, and those who cannot change their minds cannot change anything." Some people believe that a leader will appear weak if he changes his mind about an important matter. While it is important to be steadfast in one's convictions, it is equally important to be able to reevaluate and make changes when appropriate.

The astronomer Copernicus set forth the controversial idea of a sun-centered universe. Until that time people believed that the sun and the planets revolved around the earth. Copernicus changed his own view of the solar system, which started a scientific revolution. Abraham Lincoln was also controversial when he changed his mind about whether or not the Constitution allowed him to sign the Emancipation Proclamation. He ultimately came to the conclusion that he should do so, putting an end to the terrible and regrettable practice of slavery. Putting an end to slavery was one of Lincoln's most important accomplishments.

Mikhail Gorbachev changed his mind about Communism. He traveled around the former Soviet Union and realized that his people were depressed and suffering. He knew that their current form of government was failing, and that Communism should come to an end. Democracy took hold and the Berlin Wall came down. Because Mikhail Gorbachev stopped supporting Communist rule, Russia and Eastern European countries are free.

While it is good to stick by your principles, one should be willing to make changes for the better. Copernicus, Lincoln and Gorbachev are good examples of great people who have changed their minds, thereby improving the world.

This is a level "4" essay. The writer uses a chronological range of good examples to illustrate how change has benefited humanity. Despite having evidence for the argument, the essay lacks organization and thus makes the flow of ideas awkward. For example, the second paragraph should be divided into two distinct paragraphs. Transitions between paragraphs would also make the ideas more clearly related.

Level "2" essay for the same topic:

The great author George Bernard Shaw observed: "Progress is impossible without change, and those who cannot change their minds cannot change anything." Some people believe that a leader will appear weak if he changes his mind about an important matter, but a leader is actually strong if he does.

Copernicus got the new idea that the planets go around the sun, not the earth. Copernicus changed his view and the center of the solar system got moved. Because we have the technology that Copernicus didn't have, it is easier for us to change one's mind.

Abraham Lincoln changed his mind about an important issue. Lincoln changed his mind about whether or not the government should stop slavery. If Lincoln did not change his mind, we might still except slavery in America. But other leaders such as Martin Luther King probably would have to change America's mind about evils like slavery.

Our world would be very lost without change. However, without change from the past, we might find solutions using the knowledge of present day leaders and technology. Sometimes change happens by chance, but in the end, we will find a way.

This is a level "2" essay. Organization is fair, but sentence structure is often awkward and there are some grammatical and usage errors. The essay is flawed in content and development. The essay is generally confusing because the thesis does not closely match the arguments presented in the essay; the second halves of the body paragraphs suggest the possibility that changes would have eventually happened regardless of the leaders who implemented them. The conclusion fails to reiterate what was stated in the introduction. Choice of vocabulary is unsophisticated.

Sample Essay Prompt #2:

Robert Frost wrote:
"Two roads diverged in a wood, and I –
I took the one less traveled by,
And that has made all the difference."

It has been said that our lives are largely the result of a series of choices we have made, some of which are associated with taking significant risks. Discuss an important choice (made by you or by someone else) that involved taking a risk. What effect did this decision have? What do you believe would have been the result if a different choice had been made?

Level "6" essay for this topic:

I'm not sure how I got the courage to join the tennis team in the 10th grade, but it was the best decision I have made thus far in my life. When I joined, I was moderately overweight, had relatively low self-esteem, and had few friends. I would be the same way now if I had not played tennis. Playing competitive tennis taught me to be physically and socially confident, committed, and eager to try new things.

Joining my high school tennis team produced a chain of successes. The first success was a physical one. Although practices included physically grueling drills, I stayed on the team because I noticed that I was getting into shape. I lost weight and felt better about my physical appearance. As the season progressed, practice became less strenuous as my aerobic endurance developed. I ran significantly faster during exercises, and I didn't tire as easily as I had earlier in the season. My physical fitness inevitably boosted my self-esteem, which in turn boosted my sense of belonging on the team.

During practice and games, I built close relationships with my coach and teammates, which encouraged me to stay on the team. Even when I lost a game, my teammates were always supportive. They would stay to cheer me on at the end of long matches, giving me the mental strength to keep pushing myself against an opponent. When I moved up to the varsity level my junior year, I had enough experience to help train both new junior varsity and varsity players. I found it rewarding that the new players felt comfortable enough to ask me for help. "Your backhand is good! Can you show me how you do it?" a freshman would ask. I was pleased to show teammates how to practice various strategies in the serve, volley, and placement. My progress, efforts, and team contributions were recognized when I won the team's Most Valuable Player award at the end of my second season. The honor of receiving this award was the peak of my tennis career.

My accomplishments on the tennis team gave me the confidence to pursue other sports-related opportunities. I eventually joined the swim and soccer teams where I found the familiar rewards of making new friends and staying in shape. The feeling of self-improvement when I swam was great, even when I dove incorrectly or was the last swimmer in a race. During the last season in soccer, I had finally scored not only one goal, but two goals in the last game! As a result of participating in other sports, I was physically active year-round and was able to maintain a healthy body image. My successes, though sometimes small, showed me that commitment to these teams was worth the effort.

My positive interactions with new people and sports would not have been possible without my rewarding experiences on the tennis team. Because tennis has shaped my physical, social, and, consequently, my emotional self, I'm now ready to pursue even more exciting challenges.

This is a level "6" essay. It is clear and focused. The introduction outlines what tennis taught the writer: confidence, commitment, and enthusiasm to try new things. Each of the following paragraphs then illustrates these points using specific details and examples. For example, the writer describes the supportive relationship with teammates during matches. The writer uses words such as "consequently" and "as a result of" to make a flowing and logical essay. The writer also uses simple and complex sentences and a varied vocabulary to make the writing interesting.

Level "4" essay for the same topic:

I'm not sure how I got the courage to join the tennis team in the 10th grade but it was the best decision I have made thus far in my life. My life would not be the same way now if I had not played tennis.

Although practices included physically grueling drills, I stayed on the team because I noticed that I was getting more fit. I was losing weight and feeling happier about how my body looked. My physical fitness inevitably boosted my self-esteem, which helped me feel an important part of the team.

During practice and games, I built relationships with my coach and teammates. I was encouraged to stay on the team. Even when I lost a game, my team would always be supportive. When I moved up to the varsity level my junior year, I had enough experience to help out both the junior varsity and varsity players. It felt good to know that the new players were comfortable enough to ask me for help. It was motivating to contribute my share of points during competitions. Though we didn't win an awful lot of games, I always felt that our scores would have been worst if I hadn't played.

My positive interactions with new people would not have been possible without my rewarding experiences on the tennis team. Because tennis has shaped my physical, social, and my emotional self, I'm now ready to pursue more exciting challenges.

This is a level "4" essay. It is fairly clear and insightful; however, the supporting ideas, particularly in the third paragraph, are too general and do not flow together to develop a coherent point. The essay's organization is unclear because the introduction does not include a developed thesis statement. There are also some minor errors in grammar and usage that detract from a superior essay.

Level "2" essay for the same topic:

The most important choice I made was joining the tennis team. I was involved in school. I was also in good shape and I made a lot of friends. If I didn't join, I would not have been involved in school.

After I joined the tennis team, I had something to do after school. I wasn't bored, and I got in shape because of the exercise. I became a more healthy person. More students should try out for sports because one should be involved with your school.

After I joined the tennis team, I met many new people. You don't get to meet different people in your classes because your in the same grade, but on the team there are many different people. For example, there are people from 9th grade up to 12th grade on the junior varsity team. I would not have met them if I wasn't on the tennis team.

Being on the tennis team was an important choice because I would have missed out on a rewarding experience. Like they say, "If you snooze, you loose."

This is a level "2" essay. Although the essay shows some organization in the introduction and the body paragraphs, the author does not include specific details or examples to make this a well-developed essay. The lack of concrete details and lack of variety in sentence structure also make the argument too general and bland. There are also frequent grammatical errors and some spelling errors. The final sentence is an attempt to make a lasting impression on the reader, but it is a cliché that does not suit the topic.

✓ Writing – Essay Strategy #14:
•   Practice, Practice, Practice

To improve your writing, you must write. Practice writing several 25-minute essays in response to the prompts below. When you begin, utilize the "five paragraph essay outline" provided on pages 170 – 171. Make photocopies of these pages for repeated use. After writing two or three essays using the outline, take the training wheels off the bike and try writing without it. You can do it! Practice makes perfect!

Practice Essay Prompts

State your position with respect to the following topics or issues. You may agree or disagree with the prompt, but state your position clearly. Provide support for your position with appropriate examples drawn from personal experience, literature, history, science and other fields.

1.   As time passes, technology advances but civilization declines.

2.   Is the quality of human life as we know it today indebted more to the arts or to the sciences?

3.   Our responses to the challenges we face become the bedrock of our character.

4.   "Imagination is more important than knowledge." *(Albert Einstein)*

5.   "He who rejects change is the architect of decay. The only human institution which rejects progress is the cemetery." *(Harold Wilson)*

6.   "Necessity is the mother of invention." *(Irish Proverb)*

7.   "Failure is, in a sense, the highway to success." *(John Keats)*

8.   "All that is necessary for the triumph of evil is that good men do nothing." *(Edmund Burke)*

9.   "All that glitters is not gold." *(Latin Proverb)*

10.   "Great spirits have always found violent opposition from mediocre minds." *(Albert Einstein)*

11.   "There is nothing to fear but fear itself." *(Franklin D. Roosevelt)*

12.   "Genius is ninety-nine percent perspiration and one percent inspiration." *(Thomas Edison)*

13.   "Any change, even a change for the better, is always accompanied by drawbacks and discomforts." *(Arnold Bennett)*

14.   There are no accidents.

15.   "A house divided against itself cannot stand." *(The Bible)*

16.   "Experience is the best teacher." *(Latin Proverb)*

17.   "A chain is no stronger than its weakest link." *(Sir Leslie Stephen)*

18.   Mistakes are doorways to discovery.

19.   "Every man is the architect of his own fortune." *(Appius)*

20.   "Virtue is not knowing but doing." *(Japanese Proverb)*

SAT ESSAY SCORING RUBRIC

	6 (OUTSTANDING)	5 (EFFECTIVE)	4 (ADEQUATE)	3 (INADEQUATE)	2 (DEFICIENT)	1 (IMPAIRED)
Overview	• Writing is explicit • Very few errors	• Writing is competent • Few errors	• Writing evidences capability • Some errors	• Writing is unsatisfactory in certain respects • Noticeably lacking in at least one of the four areas below	• Writing is substandard • Significantly lacking in at least one and usually two or more of the four areas below	• Writing is significantly flawed • Seriously lacking in two or more of the four areas below
Support & Development	• Insightful argument is supported by explicit and reasonable examples • Ideas persuasively elaborate upon and develop argument	• Clear argument is supported by reasonable examples • Almost all examples effectively illustrate argument	• Position possesses adequate but not advanced reasoning • Utilizes some examples to support argument	• Argument is limited • Examples are undeveloped	• Argument is weak and undeveloped • Examples are limited, inappropriate or ineffective	• Argument is absent or haphazard • Has no relevant examples
Organization	• Clear and focused ideas logically flow together • Varied sentences are effectively constructed	• Ideas are focused and flow together • Has different kinds of sentence formations	• Ideas are generally easy to follow • Has some different sentence combinations	• Argument is inconsistent, yet somewhat easy to follow • Most sentences follow similar structures	• Argument is inconsistent and difficult to follow • Shows difficulties with sentence construction	• Ideas are disorganized and form no logical structure • Shows chronic difficulties with sentence construction
Language & Vocabulary	• Diction is effective and diverse	• Diction is suitable	• Diction is somewhat appropriate	• Language is sometimes bland or inappropriate	• Language is often ineffective or unsuitable	• Word choice is generally vague or incorrect
Grammar, Usage & Mechanics	• Has very few (if any) minor errors in observing the conventions of standard written English	• Has few overall errors in observing the conventions of standard written English	• Contains some errors in usage and mechanics	• Contains several grammatical or usage errors	• Errors in grammar, usage and mechanics are considerable • Phrases are difficult to follow	• Shows widespread deficiency in observing the conventions of standard written English • Phrases are often incoherent

About the Author

Lisa Muehle is a co-founder and director of Cambridge Academic Services & Consulting, Inc., Laguna Beach, California. Ms. Muehle originated the *Colloquium Test Prep Course for the SAT*, a long term SAT training program for 7th – 11th grade students, in 1992. Three of Ms. Muehle's students have posted perfect SAT scores. Because of the unique long-term nature of the Colloquium program and its phenomenal score results, Lisa Muehle and the *Colloquium Test Prep Course for the SAT* have received extensive media coverage, including:

- *PBS Frontline* documentary "Secrets of the SAT" (aired Oct. 5, 1999)
- *CBS Early Show* feature "Kids and the SAT" (aired May 2, 2002)
- Los Angeles Times half-page feature in the Metro section, "Scoring SAT Tutors" (published October 12, 1998)
- USA Today editorial (published July 11, 2000)
- Orange County Register front-page feature article, "For SAT, Even Young Teens Know the Score" (published January 31, 2004)

978-1-58348-478-4
1-58348-478-7